THE SAUCERS SPEAK

CALLING ALL OCCUPANTS OF INTERPLANETARY CRAFT

George Hunt Williamson
aka Brother Philip

With Alfred Bailey
Timothy Green Beckley
And Sean Casteel

THE SAUCERS SPEAK
CALLING ALL OCCUPANTS OF INTERPLANETARY CRAFT

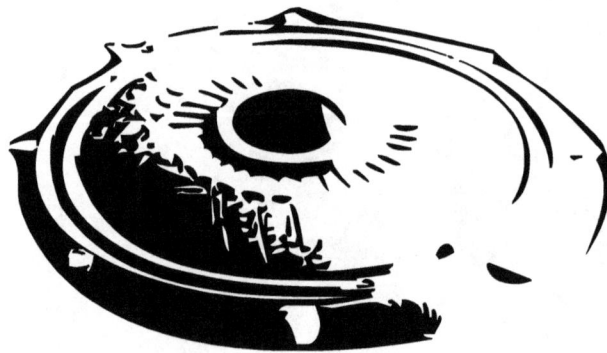

THE SAUCERS SPEAK

CALLING ALL OCCUPANTS OF INTERPLANETARY CRAFT

A Documentary Report
of
Interstellar Communication by Radiotelegraphy
by
George Hunt Williamson—1963

ISBN-10: 1606111329
ISBN-13: 9781606111321

Timothy Green Beckley: Editorial Director
Carol Rodriguez: Publisher's Assistant
Associate Editors: Sean Casteel and Tim Swartz
Special Thanks: William Kern

For Free Subscription To The Conspiracy Journal Write:

Tim Beckley · Box 753
New Brunswick, NJ 08903

Sign Up Online: MRUFO8@hotmail.com
www.ConspiracyJournal.Com
www.TeslaSecretLab.Com

CONTENTS

ABOUT THE AUTHOR

George Hunt Williamson was, above all, a Seeker. From an early age he came under influences which, whether by chance or fate or design, propelled his life into a search for answers to the events of his inner and outer life.

In his late teens when Williamson followed the inner urge to discover the answers to his many questions he did what many do- sought the nearest so called 'experts' he could find. Unfortunately this lead him into the confused and murky world of Pelley and his associates and their theories and dogma coloured his thinking and ongoing research for many years. However, even in SoulCraft's distorted mythology were Pearls of wisdom and guidance taken from older sources and these were digested by Williamson and worked their magic in his inner world and subconscious. Williamson was honest in his Search- he was not going to settle for the half hearted and the spurious and he moved on from these early influences, - he carried on his search into the future with even more energy.

The dramatic increase in UFO awareness in the late forties and early fifties resonated very deeply with Williamson, because in his childhood he had had personal experiences through dreams and physical reality with the UFO archetype and phenomenon. Of course at that time UFO's were unknown and so Williamson had to place his experiences in the more 'conventional' mythologies available to him. But when the UFO's began to increase their presence in the skies above, Williamson immediately realised that somehow he was a part of it- that he was personally connected with the UFO phenomenon.

This lead him to a deep study of the mythology from the indigenous peoples of his American homeland and then South America. Along the way he, of course, dabbled in 'mainstream' ufology, he saw the UFO's as physical spaceships from elsewhere and attempted contact with them- he wrote books about his early experiments with ham radio and so on. But all the while Williamson's own Search- to discover answers to his own inner questions, to understand himself – continued, deepened, became more sincere. He knew that his experiments, writings, and his connections with people such as Adamski were not the answer- Williamson was aways left, finally alone with himself and his own Question unanswered.

Suddenly, in the early sixties, George Hunt Williamson disappeared from public view.

Willamson had left to discover his destiny in South America, and for him and his own personal quest this lead to the answers and understandings he had searched for, his entire life. Outwardly he authored his most famous, and for many, inspired books- filled with wonderful mythologies weaving together all the threads he had discovered along the way- but these were not his truth, his personal truth- they were written for the world in allegorical form, he wrote from inspiration and his books were designed to carry certain information in a coded pattern into the future. That is why the author of these books is given as Brother Philip rather than George Hunt Williamson.

In South America Williamson finally "met" with the consciousness behind the UFO's and phenomenon which had been such a part of his entire lifes story and the truth he discovered led to the ending of his UFO research, rather than a new beginning. He had found himself.

Upon returning to the U.S., Williamson lead a much 'quieter' and private life, though he still researched into earth mysteries and so on his main inclination was to follow the path of a type of, for him, true Christian way in the Gnostic tradition.

Behold a fairer time is with you than any men have dreamed of; behold there is gladness again in the heavens when a host not of earth is seen of all shepherds.

High in open heavens, a new Host rusheth unto you; it singeth of beauties whose eagerness greeteth you;

There is a new trumpet and an excellent tongue to voice it; there is a new paean and a stronger throat to roll it, there is a high summoning and yet a new joy that Man perceiveth to surfeit the threats to darkened infinities.

These things a new Host voiceth, and their silver hath a trade-stamp that rebuketh man's incredulence.

—From *The Golden Scripts*

〰〰 **Mountain Ranges**

○ **Lunar Craters**

✳ **Blinking Lights**

✰ **Star-like Lights**

∥∥ **Streaks of Light**

INTRODUCTION

In the first edition of this book, published in America in 1954, the radio operator who received signals from space remained anonymous. He was referred to as Mr. "R," a radioman. Since his first experiments, many other operators have been inspired to attempt radio contact with the intelligence behind the UFO. In 1955, a Canadian official wrote to me and informed me that Canadian radio operators had successfully communicated with the same space group that had originally contacted Mr. R in Arizona.

The radio messages are printed in SMALL CAPITAL letters for easy identification. In some cases, the messages were in a code not understood by the radio operator or witnesses present. Therefore, they are reproduced exactly as received. Some of these unknown messages seem to be part of a two-way communication between space ships, others are nothing more than reports between very earthly ships at sea.

In this edition, Mr. R is revealed as Mr. Lyman H. Streeter, W7OJQ, a radio operator for the Santa Fe Railroad. Photographs of his home and radio ham shack in Winslow, are reproduced here for the first time. This edition is enlarged with the addition of the chapter, *Mr. R's Secret,* and the chapter, *Cosmic Rays and a Baby Sun.*

At the end of this edition, you will find the Merint Programme radiotelegraph procedure sheet (authorized by the Secretary of the Navy, USA). This is the first time it has been copied or published anywhere, since the United States wants apparently to keep knowledge of Merint from private citizens. The programme is used by USA and Canadian Merchant Vessels (coastwise) "for early warning in defense of the North American continent." The radiotelegraph sheet is to be posted in the radio room and on the bridge of every ship. It bears the designation: OPNAV $_{94}$-P-$_3$B (there is a similar sheet, OPNAV $_{94}$-P-$_3$A, that is used for radiotelephone procedure).

The reader will notice the statement: "Report immediately all airborne and waterborne objects which appear to be hostile, suspicious or are unidentified." The perfect drawing of an UFO is interesting.

The American government is aware that UFOs exist (proven by recent statements in the House of Representatives), *how much* they know about them is another matter.

Recently, a well-known "Saucer" author wrote a book titled *Flying Saucers Farewell.* I rather doubt the idea that UFOs have gone home again. They have been surveying us for thousands of years and they will not leave until their programme is culminated. Farewell, indeed? They are still being seen daily all over the world. The little group of researchers in Arizona in 1952 opened the way for radio contact with space. When will the governments of the world continue that pioneering effort? Only time will tell, and there isn't too much of that left.

GEORGE HUNT WILLIAMSON

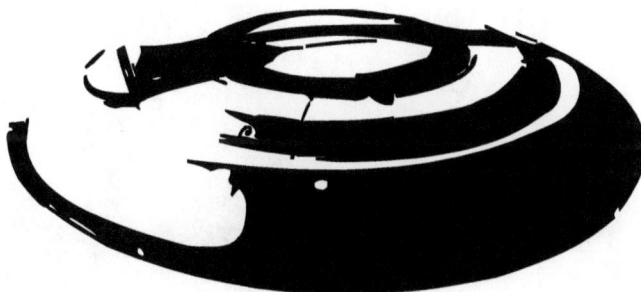

Williamson's interests spanned many subjects. He was also an avid archaeological buff who traveled widely and authored such controversial works as *Road in the Sky* and *Secret of the Andes and the Golden Disc of Mu.*

From a distance, Williamson says he saw UFO contactee George Adamski standing face-to-face with a being from another planet who looked remarkably human. Adamski later said this individual was from Venus and had identified himself as Orthon. They communicated via telepathy. (Illustration by Gene Duplantier).

UFOs were appearing on a regular bases in the skies above California in the late 1940s and 1950s. It was photographs such as this one by George Adamski that attracted the author to the flying saucer mystery.

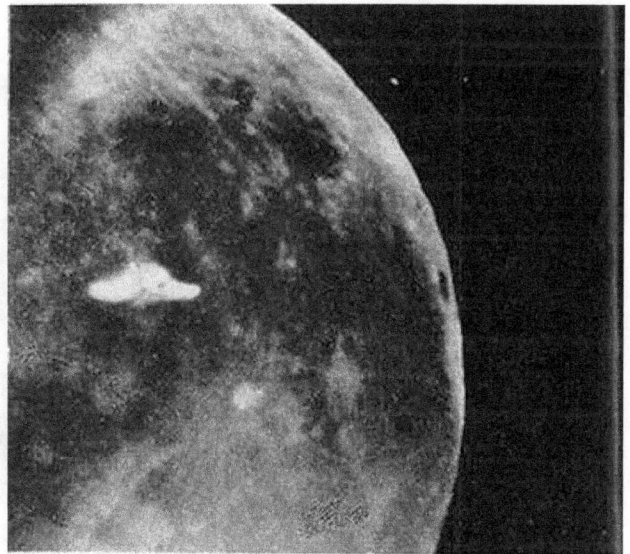

A similar craft seen by Adamski through his telescope passing between earth and the moon. 2.30 a.m., June 6, 1950

1

Giant Rock Interplanetary Spacecraft Convention April 1954

A very youthful looking Williamson on the far right must have felt light headed as he was surrounded by those he admired who claimed to have encountered space beings and who said they had been taken on board the craft popularly known as flying saucers.

Speakers included (from left) Orfeo Angelucci (Secret of the Saucers), George Van Tassel (Integratron), Frank Scully (columnist), and George Hunt Williamson (Road in the Sky)

Williamson leads a group in attempting to communicate with the occupants of flying saucers. The author says he successfully spoke with beings from other worlds.

PROBING THE MYSTERY OF THE
UNEXPLAINABLE RADIO TRANSMISSIONS

By Timothy Green Beckley

Since the 1950s, the FCC, as well as other governmental agencies, have been checking out reports of mysterious interference over various broadcast frequencies. Whether it's a powerful TV station in England, high frequency channels reserved strictly for astronaut communication, ham set or CB equipment, some unknown sources of intelligence have the ability to 'cut in' and take over the airwaves as they see fit.

You probably read a brief wire service account of the incident in your local newspaper. The authorities tried to explain the "voice from outer space" as the work of a practical joker who had somehow managed to take control of an abandoned transmitter and broadcast a message from the "Asteron Galactic Command." They made it seem like the broadcast had lasted only a matter of 30 seconds or so, while in reality there were several messages, not just one, all of which lasted for a good two or three minutes apiece.

The following is a complete transcript of the "voice from outer space" as broadcast on television in the Hennington area of Southern England at 5:05 PM on Saturday, November 26, 1977. This is the first time the text of the broadcast has been published in its entirety in the United States:

The Incredible Message

"This is the voice of Glon, representative of the Asteron Galactic Command, speaking to you. For many years you have seen us as lights in the sky. We speak to you now in peace and wisdom as we have done to your brothers and sisters all over this, your planet Earth.

"We come to warn you of the destiny of your race in your world so that you may communicate to your fellow beings the course you must take to avoid disaster which threatens your world and the beings of other worlds around you.

"This is in order that you may share in the great awakening as the planet passes

3

into the New Age of Aquarius. The New Age can be a time of great evolution for your race, but only if your rulers are made aware of the evil forces that can overshadow their judgment. Be still now, and listen, for your chance may not come again for many years.

"Your scientists, governments and generals have not heeded our warnings. They have continued to experiment with the evil forces of what you call nuclear energy. Atomic bombs can destroy the Earth and the beings of your sister worlds in a moment. The wastes from atomic power systems will poison your planet for many thousands of years to come. We who have followed the path of evolution for far longer than you, have long since realized this, that atomic energy is always directed against life. It has no peaceful application. Its use and research into its use must be ceased at once, or you will all risk destruction. All weapons of evil must be removed.

"The time of conflict is now passed and the races of which you are a part may proceed to the highest planes of evolution, if you show yourselves worthy to do this. You have but a short time to learn to live together in peace and good will. Small groups all over the planet are learning this and exist to pass on the light of a new dawning, the New Age to you all. You are free to accept or reject their teachings, but only those who learn to live in peace will pass to the higher realms of spiritual evolution.

"Hear then the voice of Glon, the voice of the Asteron Galactic Command speaking to you. Be aware also that there are many false prophets and guides at present operating on your world. They will suck your energy from you, the energy you call money, and will put it to evil ends, giving you worthless gross in return. Your inner divine self will protect you from this. You must learn to be sensitive to the voice within that can tell you what is truth and what is confusion, chaos and untruth. Learn to listen to the voice of truth which is within you and you will lead yourself onto the path of evolution.

"This is our message to you, our dear friends. We have watched you growing for many years, just as you have watched our lights in the skies. You know now that we are here and that there are more beings on and around your Earth than your scientists care to admit. We are deeply concerned about you and your path towards the light and we will do all we can to help you. Have no fears, seek only to know yourself and live in harmony with the ways of your planet Earth.

"We are the Asteron Galactic Command. Thank you for your attention. We are now leaving the planes of your existence. May you be blessed with supreme love and truth of the cosmos.

The Unperturbed British

If there is one thing most Britishers have in common, it's their unflappability. They've lived through the blitz, survived more Channel storms than you can count, and taken every imaginable type of man or nature-spawned excess very much in stride.

That's why they felt prepared to ride out any bad new which was transmitted to them over their regularly scheduled newscasts of November 26. But in homes all over Hampshire County, and as far north as Reading in Berkshire and Witney in Oxfordshire,

TV viewers got the shock of their lives and caused the usually unflappable Britons to jam the switchboards of every police station for miles around. Voices from space are not your usual evening's entertainment.

According to those who live in the area, towards the end of Southern Television's evening news program, a series of "bleeps" gradually took over the normal sound.

Commented one viewer, "It was the kind of signal you get prior to a bulletin of special importance." Following the bleeps, a voice cut into the regular broadcast frequency of the TV station.

Another segment that came in was as follows:

The New Message

"We speak to the people of the planet Earth. It is of great importance that you have the understanding that we come only in love and peace. It is a time of importance in the universe that the planet Earth be invoked and the consciousness of those that exist on the planet be raised to a higher degree. It is also important to you to understand that we cannot permit in the present nor in the future, any more devastation upon Earth.

"There are those civilizations that are in service to the universe that are in motion to come to your planet Earth to give mankind the benefit of their medical and technological skills, but mainly of their love. They are in service to the planet Earth and to the universe. We conveyed to Sir John Whitmore and to the Dr. Puharich that we would interfere on your radio and television communication systems to relay when the civilizations are coming close to landing on your planet.

"It is now in motion. We wish you to know that we love you. We wish for there not to be panic on Earth, for we come in peace. But it is also important for the people of Earth to recognize that the civilizations that come, come in Brotherhood to help them. It is important now to become one with the Brotherhood of the universe. We ask that those of Earth do not attempt to prevent the civilizations that are coming, but to accept them in love as we have accepted the planet Earth in love even though it has caused devastation and in turn contaminated the universe. We are with you and we come in peace."

A Fast Reaction

According to viewer Rex Monger, "The voice seemed to suggest that the man was speaking from a spacecraft traveling within the vicinity of Earth. He sounded pretty fed up with the way we are running things down here."

As usually happens in such cases, a spokesman for Southern Television offered the typical debunking statements, calling the transmission "a pretty sick hoax" and likening it to the 1938 Orson Welles radio adaptation of H.G. Well's "War of the Worlds." But as the days went on, the station was forced to admit that it had gathered no actual evidence that the transmission had indeed been a hoax. The official said, "Our engineers are trying to discover exactly what happened. We can't imagine how it was done, but it appears someone must have managed to transmit a signal directly over ours. The equipment used would need to be fairly sophisticated and expensive."

A Chilling Message

The mysterious November English transmission fits into an overall pattern of such events which have been occurring on a world-wide basis over the last several decades.

While the official stance of such government agencies as the Federal Communications Commission remains that such transmissions are a hoax, in no case has any prosecution been brought, much less a conviction obtained. This even though there are strong communications laws on the books making such transmissions a Federal offense.

Nor can debunkers explain away the fact that witnesses to the receipt of such transmissions are highly reputable people not given to fantasizing or bouts of hysteria. Included in their ranks are a number of law enforcement officers as well as several astronauts.

The transmissions have come over commercial frequencies, citizens' bands and high frequency channels reserved for communicating in outer space.

Of particular interest is the fact that while some transmissions have been in unrecognizable code and others in unintelligible language, a good many messages have been broadcast in the colloquial dialect of the area.

Alien Robot Communicates

A good example of this is provided by a tape in the possession of this author of an actual transmission received by a night guard employed by the Alamac Knitting Mills located in Lumberton, North Carolina.

To set the scene for the experience of James Ed Floyd, Alamac's night security guard, we must turn back to early April, 1975, and the area around Lumberton.

Lumberton is in the southeastern section of the state. It is flat with heavy patches of pine forests, open areas of farmland, swamps and canals. On April 5th, 1975, Lumberton became the focal point of UFO investigators when the first in a series of sightings of a V-shaped object in the sky was reported.

On the nights which followed an untold number of sightings were funneled through various police stations. Forty-eight of the actual sightings were attributed to police officers engaged in official business.

The first inkling that the UFO must have been bent on jamming radio frequencies in the Lumberton environs came when at 2:28 AM, April 3rd, Officer Jim Driver of the Roseboro (Sampson County) Police Department, alone in his patrol car, noticed a series of lights in the sky hovering over some pecan trees. This was the third sighting of the night, but the importance of it was that Driver became the first lawman to tell of the object's interference with his radio transmission.

Said Driver, "I got out of the car at that point and could not hear any sound coming from the object. When I tried to radio headquarters my car radio became all scrambled, so I had to use my walkie-talkie instead. The light on the object swung away and lit up the pecan trees which were about 200 feet away.

As more and more sightings were made known within the next hour, Lumberton authorities immediately contacted the Center for UFO Studies, with headquarters in Evanston, Illinois. Expert investigator Lee Spiegel was dispatched to North Carolina.

Hollow Voice

As part of his ongoing probe, Spiegel interviewed Floyd. Floyd said that not only had he experienced numerous sightings of the UFO, but that he had heard a strange hollow-sounding voice over his CB radio. The voice described itself as "Robot." It indicated that it was broadcasting over South Carolina, but was heading north.

Spiegel notes that Floyd's story seemed to be corroborated by information that as the unexplained radio signal from "Robot" became stronger, other residents of the Lumberton area found their radios being jammed to such a degree that offices could no longer modulate with each other.

In his official report to the Center for UFO Studies, Spiegel notes that Floyd told him that the voice, which spoke with a Carolina drawl had said that it could not speak with them or be seen after dawn.

Spiegel suggested that Floyd try to record the voice on a tape cassette recorder. The plan was put into operation, and on Sunday, April 12th between 7:00 AM and 7:15, the recording was made.

Spiegel has provided the author with the tape, and although the quality is not good, certain phrases are decipherable.

"Robot We are clear.. .we may be in violation of rules. You may be violating the rules and regulations of the 'National Loudmouth...by modulating with this one Robot. We may be violating..."

Floyd (speaking back on the radio): "You're breaking some rules, right? Right, you are!"

Robot: "Do not modulate with this one, Robot. . . we are circling around and checking our difference, and they do not like for any voice to modulate with this one Robot.

"We are not black, we are not white, we are not red, we are not yellow, we are not anything...We are just one Robot, we are circling for the pleasure of our commanding vehicle. Anybody that does not like the sound RRRR-RRRRRR of this one Robot..."

After Floyd arrived at his home, the voice was still transmitting and Floyd's son typed up the following words of a CB unit in their home.

"We are not.. .anybody. .that we did from out there...we are not a computer, but we are a Robot, we are computerized...

"We do... take the Earthling's words and twist it around and turn it against..."

Some months later, Floyd claimed he heard another broadcast by the same voice, and then the UFOs vanished from the area and the eerie-sounding voice right along with it.

UFO Zaps Texas Hams

Another case of the interference with normal radio communications occurred in Calvert, Texas, during a siege by UFOs. The small southwest community was flooded by transmissions of radio sounds with a regular cadence which might have been some alien code. The transmissions peaked in November of 1973, corresponding with the brunt of the UFO sighting wave.

Ham radio operator and television repairman Virgil Chappel notes, "Almost every night during the early part of November, heavy interference plagued amateur broadcasters in the area, preventing us from communicating with one another as we regularly do. Instead of hearing the normal messages from fellow hams, all I could pick up was a series of clicks. They were closely akin to Morse Code. Being somewhat of an expert in codes, however, I can vouch for the fact that it was decisively different from anything I had heard before. Why, even the tonal pitch of the 'noise' was odd, varying greatly from high to low. It was definitely—as far as I'm concerned—an intelligent type of signal. I don't profess to know where it came from, and I don't know who was behind it. All I can positively state is that it was eerie to listen to!"

On November 15th, 1973, the stocky Texan received an additional jolt of "eeriness" when he ventured out into his backyard and was greeted by the sight of a series of lights. "The air all around was aglow with a multitude of twinkling lights. It was like a Christmas tree-that's about the best way I can describe the scene. All around and above me were these blinking spheres. I ran inside the house, yelled to my wife to follow me back outside and simultaneously grabbed a pair of binoculars which I thought would give me a better view of what I was certain were not airplanes, stars, or those satellites that come over every so often."

Chappel was unable to determine the actual shape of the objects but nevertheless was bedazzled by the beautiful hues of light they emitted.

Senator Goldwater

No less a famous person than Senator Barry Goldwater claims he has heard strange signals on his ham radio set. "These signals had a cadence or sequence which sounded like a code," he has stated. "It wasn't like any code I'd ever heard before. The U.S. and the other countries like Russia have picked up such signals. But nobody knows where they come from or what they are. I do know that NASA is doing a lot of research into this."

Contacts between operators of unknown frequencies and hams are on the rise. David L. Dobbs, a Cincinnati scientist, gives a graphic description of just such an encounter in a communique written to Walt Andrus, director of the prestigious Mutual UFO Network.

A Close Encounter Set Up Via the Airwaves

Dobbs says he was driving home late at night on August 12th, 1976 and was monitoring a ham call in which the operator was trying to give directions to a mobile which was lost. As Dobbs was awaiting the "repeater" on the message, the voice was suddenly cut off. The engine of Dobbs's car began to miss and his headlights started to flicker. Although the electrical system of his vehicle returned to normal within split seconds, the receiver remained silent.

"Hoping the rig was OK, I identified for autopatch and punched the access code," Dobbs says. "They tell me that no one monitoring heard a thing, but instead of the dial tone, there was this indescribable voice.

"'Priority Break,' it intoned, followed by some strange call mobile 8. Usually I remember calls, but the odd quality of that voice must have distracted me. It was kind of melodious, deep and compelling, with an accent I couldn't place. I just said, 'Go break,' and kept listening. From that point on, the whole incident had a sort of dreamlike quality.

"The fascinating voice went on to say that his vehicle was disabled on old Route 84 near the quarry and requested some assistance. It was my impression that he was probably some foreign ham operating on a reciprocal license. The nationality escaped me, but as a technician I don't work the low bands, and there are a lot of new countries these days.

"Since my OTH was only a few miles from him, I told him to standby and I would be there as soon as possible."

Dobbs traveled the highway to the intersection with 84, turned into the ancient road whose decrepit pavement forced him to reduce his speed to 15 or 20 miles an hour.

After going some distance, the scientist found his way blocked by a fallen branch. He stopped his car and got out in order to remove the obstacle. It was then that he noticed the treetops some 200 yards away were illuminated by a flickering light. It was as if something might be burning, except that the light had a bluish tint, something like that made by the rotating flasher of a police car.

Approaches The Spaceman

"And then suddenly I saw him," Dobbs continues. "Him seems to fit somehow, but don't ask me why. He had come up for the car while my back was turned and was standing near the open door. In the glare of the headlights it was hard to see well, but he was short—probably not five feet in height. He had on a silvery one-piece outfit that looked like aluminized coveralls or a wet suit. Moving out of the headlight beams and towards the car, I was about to say, 'Hi,' when my first good looked stopped me dead. He didn't have a recognizable face."

Dobbs tells how he began receiving a tremendous flow of information into his mind at a "fantastic rate."

"It was like a data link between two computers," he comments. "Ideas weren't expressed in words at all—there was just a stream of impressions."

The Cincinnati man went on for what appeared to be no more than 15 or 20 seconds. Dobbs was told he had no reason to fear his visitor and felt the figure was some sort of "biological robot." His impression was that the visitor had traveled from distant stars in this galaxy—stars which were visible only in the southern hemisphere.

Dobbs accompanied the figure to a space ship and came away with the thought that for some reason earthlings were being evaluated by the extraterrestrials.

He is also sure that the humanoid borrowed a package Dobbs was carrying at the time in order to duplicate its contents.

As Dobbs was returning to his own car at the suggestion of the humanoid, who had indicated that to be close to the UFO at the moment of its take-off might prove hazardous, he became aware of the spacecraft hovering overhead. A moment later it flew off in a tremendous burst of speed.

Tampering With Our Space Program

Strange and inexplicable as the radio and television contacts between private citizens and space aliens may be, they are nowhere near as bizarre as those which have occurred between those engaged in scientific experimentation and space exploration as government representatives and possible representatives from outer space.

On November 23rd, 1977, officials at Cape Canaveral, Florida were forced to admit that they were launching an all-out probe into the origin of a mysterious series of radio signals which had forced the scrubbing of a launch of a Meteorite I satellite.

Spokesmen for the Air Force and National Aeronautics and Space Administration revealed that the unexplained radio signals had been discovered during a routine check of the rocket's electrical system.

While the investigators pressed their efforts to unravel the mystery, the 1,535 pound drum-shaped satellite which is owned by the European Space Agency, sat on the ground and the $240 million Meteosat weather forecasting program remained stalled.

The cryptic word from Canaveral was, "The source of the signals must be determined before a new launch date can be set because they could have an effect on the destruct system."

In jeopardy was a "World Weather Watch" experiment in which European, Japanese and American satellites were to participate.

Mysterious Voices Overide Skylab Transmission

Nor was this the first time that the space program was rattled by a so-called "space phantom." On February 19th, 1974, noted syndicated columnist and muckraker Jack Anderson reported that "mysterious voices" had imperiled the return to earth of Skylab III with its crew.

According to Anderson's account, Skylab's crew heard mysterious voices telling of an explosion over Moscow, an oxygen loss and a conversation with then President Nixon. Anderson considered the transmissions an elaborate hoax and noted that an all-out probe was underway towards apprehending the "perpetrator" who had violated NASA's communication frequencies. However, as in every other case of this nature, no suspect were ever rounded up nor were any formal charges ever drawn.

The facts of the incident are these:

In Rocky Mount, North Carolina, officials of Unifi, Inc., a textile firm, began having interference with a long distance call. The interference at first sounded like radio transmissions from an airliner, but later on the listeners realized they were monitoring what they thought to be a conversation between Skylab Ill and the Houston Space Center. It appeared the astronauts' side of the radio conversation was the only one being audited. The voices talked of a 10 megaton explosion over Soviet Russia observed while the Spacecraft had been taking aerial reconnaissance photographs of underground Soviet missile silos. The message included the fact that the Spacecraft had been severely damaged in the encounter and only had 11 hours oxygen supply aboard. The voices then said they were going to scramble the transmission on channels five and eight. A series of coded messages which sounded similar to Morse code ensued.

At this point, according to Anderson, the words, "Yes, Mr. President, we understand this," were heard followed by a voice report that SpaceLab's secret documents and equipment had been thrown overboard. The transmission ended there.

The executive employees of Unifi were not the only ones to hear the message. Anderson's associate Joe Spear found a number of others who had monitored the same dire conversations.

Said Anderson, "At NASA, officials advised us that still others around the country had reported similar phone interference.

"Now, NASA's security specialists are trying to find which 'phone freak' perpetrated the elaborate hoaxes. So far, we have learned only the 'Space Phantom' knows."

Despite Anderson's somewhat flip attitude, the fact remains that a number of years have passed since the incident and as yet, NASA has never officially admitted that it took place. Nor has the "perpetrator" been apprehended.

NASA Records Provide More Documentation

Strange sounds which cannot be explained away have long been a part of NASA operations. A careful check of the tapes of Apollo 12's log presents a vivid recounting of the monitoring of strange signals by American Astronauts Pete Conrad and Allan Bean. Conrad and Bean have landed on the moon's surface and were undergoing their exercise program when the following conversation took place:

Bean: Do you hear a lot of background noises, Pete?

Conrad: Kind of static and things.

Bean: I keep hearing a whistle.

Conrad: That's what I hear: O.K.

Ten minutes later, Dick Gordon in the mothership orbiting the moon reported the following to Houston control.

Gordon: Hey, Houston, do you hear this constant beep in the background?

CAPCOM :That's affirmative. We've heard it now for about the past 45 minutes.

Gordon: That's right, so have we. What is it?

Ground control could give no definition.

Nor has NASA been able to come up with a logical explanation for the unintelligible foreign language transmission heard on Gordon Cooper's fourth pass over Hawaii on Faith 7 on May 15th, 1963. It should be remembered that these channels on which the transmissions were heard had been reserved for space flights. And it should also be remembered that in the ensuing 28 years, NASA has never been able to identify the source of the transmissions nor the foreign language involved.

Another question which nobody connected with the government is able (or willing) to answer is—was there a secret warning embodied in the tune which for some unknown reason filled the cabin of Walter Schirra, Jr.'s Apollo 7. The melody was remarkably close to the old ballad "Fools Rush In Where Angels Fear To Tread." The one thing which is certain is that the song was neither being transmitted from the ground nor from Apollo 7 itself.

On Apollo 11, the sounds resembled those of fire engines and caused Mission Control to query, "You sure you don't have anybody else in there with you?" The question, posed on July 22nd, went unanswered by the crew.

The very next day at 1030 hours, the strange sounds began again. This time they resembled a train whistle and the labored chugging of a steam locomotive. NASA could not locate the source and made a joke of the fact by asking astronaut Buzz Aldren whether he might be exercising too violently. Instead of an answer, NASA's headphones were filled by other whistles and squawks which made auditing conversations extremely difficult.

Beaming In On Earth

Whether it was Asteron's warning to the British television views, the red-necked message taped in Lumberton, N.C., the experience of the Calvert, Texas ham radio operator, the Cincinnati visitation of a being which invaded CB channels or the more sophisticated incursions into the space and satellite programs, there is no denying that the evidence is all around us that our airwaves are being jammed at will by something or somebody who feels the time has come to communicate with us.

While the official line from government spokesmen remains, as it always has in the past, that such happenings are elaborately contrived hoaxes, the truth cannot be denied.

Federal law has been violated again and again. Using the most ultramodern devices in their arsenal against piracy of the airwaves, federal officials have not been able to break one case. There have been no convictions. There have been no arrests. There aren't even any viable suspects.

Until there are, those in charge are going to have to come up with a better explanation than the tired old bromide, "It's just malicious mischief."

And while such episodes of establishing some sort of communications with the occupants of "interplanetary" craft make up a sizable portion of the mystery of the Ultra-Terrestrial, very few of these cases have ever received the attention they deserve. UFO researchers have ignored them as they do many matters that could lead to important breakthroughs in this field.

But we must give credit where credit is due, for it was George Hunt Williamson who first brought up communicating with the occupants of interplanetary craft, and yet because of the controversial nature of his studies (and a rather quirky personality), his involvement in the area of Ultra-Terrestrial contact by radio has been glossed over.

Now in his own words we revive the "glory years" when the contactees reined supreme and the "Space Brothers" seemed to play a more important role in our lives.

An exceedingly rare photo of researcher/publisher Timothy Beckley (circa 1967) gazing upon a bigger than life painting of Orthon, the long haired "man from Venus," who George Adamski claims to have first made contact with in the California desert. Williamson says he was a witness to this historic encounter.

CALLING ALL OCCUPANTS OF INTERPLANETARY CRAFT

From A Lecture Given By George Hunt Williamson

On Monday, June 21, 1954 in Detroit, Michigan

It is a great privilege and pleasure to be here in Detroit to speak to you on the subject of "flying saucers." The term "flying saucers" until very recently in the world has been more laugh provoking than it has been thought provoking. But now people all over the world are beginning to realize that this phenomenon known as the "flying saucers" may have a great bearing on the lives of each and everyone of us in the not too distant future!

Tonight I will tell you of our own experiences with flying saucers. I also know of a number of men who have had various similar experiences. I was with George Adamski in November of 1952 when he had the memorable contact in the desert with the flying saucer. Both my wife and I were witnesses to that event. The event as it is described in the book entitled Flying Saucers Have Landed by Desmond Leslie and George Adamski is accurate and true. However, our work in flying saucers started long before our contact with Mr. Adamski. It was through our own work that we heard of him and eventually met him.

We wondered what to do with the information we had collected and decided to go to see George Adamski who was only 400 miles away from us. In the book Flying Saucers Have Landed, Mr. Adamski has several good pictures of saucers. The great astronomical observatories of the world also have pictures of saucers. I have a friend who went to school with one of the astronomers who is now working at the "Big Eye" (telescope) at Mount Palomar. Many times the students of various universities are allowed to spend time at the Big Observatory to work on certain projects. This friend of mine was at Mount Palomar and asked his former classmate, the astronomer, how it was that an amateur photographer like George Adamski could get pictures of saucers and Mount Palomar could not, and if Adamski's pictures were fake.

The astronomer replied that Mr. Adamski's pictures were NOT fake and if he thought Adamski's pictures were good, he should see the ones they have at Mount Palomar. The government has the story. They also have made radio contact with saucers. Whether they will ever give out this information or not we do not know. They may wait until we all know about it and then confirm it.

There is a project known as MQ707 at Edwards Air Force Base which is a project for telecommunication with saucers. They contact these craft and attempt to get them to land. In August 1952 we had our own contacts with space people via short wave or radio telegraphy. I had been in Minnesota a year or more previously where I was working among the Chippewa Indians gathering little known legends and facts about them that had not been accumulated or written down before.

I knew nothing more about saucers than most people. There had been a few things in the newspapers and I had, of course, heard of flying saucers. On the way to Minnesota I picked up a copy of Major Kehoe's first book Flying Saucers Are Real. When I arrived in Minnesota, it was raining and continued to rain for several days. I could not get out of my cabin so I read the book. Once I started it I could not put it down until I finished it. After I finished reading it I was thoroughly convinced myself that these things could at least be interplanetary.

Here was a man, a former Marine Major, who had gone into the subject in an objective way and had analyzed all the facts and had come to the conclusion that they could not be anything else but something from outer space. In fact, I believe he mentioned in the book that it was hard for him to accept this and that it was fantastic, but that no other conclusion seemed to fit the evidence. As I read this book, all the Indian legends I had been collecting seemed to fall into place, and I began to see that a number of the stories I had collected sounded like flying saucers. I checked with my wife who was doing work among the Mexican Indians and found she had been finding the same thing.

On further investigation, we found that all American Indian tribes had practically the same legends. There were slight variations but they almost all had the same basic facts. For a long time anthropologists had discarded Indian legends and the stories of so-called primitive people throughout the world because they said they were merely the stories of superstitious people and had no basis or fact. No longer are they doing this for they realize that there must be something to start a story and although these legends or stories were not written down as they did not have a written language, they were passed from generation to generation.

One of the Chippewa's legends is the account of the "Gin Guin" or the "Earth-rumblers," or the "Wheels-that-rumble-the-earth." The story in essence is this: At various times a rotating wheel or whirling wheel, sometimes surrounded by a cloud, would descend and lightning would sometimes be seen to shoot from it. Then out of it would step a young fair-haired man whom they called "Bococitti," the fair-haired god who comes from the skies. Stories like these are found throughout the United States and in fact almost all primitive people throughout the world seem to have the same kind of legends.

After I left Minnesota, I joined my wife in Prescott, Arizona, where my family lives. A friend of mine, Alfred C. Bailey, came to visit me and asked to see what I had been accumulating on my recent trip. I did not mention saucers, but let him read some of the legends. When he finished reading the material I had collected, he said: "This sounds like flying saucers. I thought your trip was to collect legends of the Indians?" We discussed the flying saucer phenomena and thought perhaps they might be weather conditions, for we would not be the first to observe weather conditions. The Indians would have seen the same things and perhaps made legends about them. We also talked about the possibility of man traveling to other planets by rockets.

One of us suggested something with a lot of "ifs" in it. If in the future we of earth planned to go to another planet, and if we found it inhabited and if they had radio or some similar type of communication, why could we not monitor their radio and attempt to learn their language and find out about the culture of the inhabitants before we landed? We decided that perhaps if the other planets were inhabited and space people were visiting us that they might now be doing this very thing. Perhaps they might even be interested in contacting certain people on earth, people who were not afraid. We were just discussing these possibilities and were really not too serious about it. We reasoned this way: If these people from outer space have been here since Kenneth Arnold first observed them in 1947, certainly they must know our language and our Morse Code communication system.

By monitoring our radios they undoubtedly could pick up our language in a short period of time, as the Morse Code System is no secret and it is used daily throughout the world. However, we decided it was all too fantastic and we then dismissed the subject.

However, several weeks afterwards Al Bailey called me and said:

"Remember what we were discussing about flying saucers? We have had success."

"What do you mean?" I asked, "Have you seen one?"

"No," he replied, "I do not mean that, I mean that we have made radio contact."

Then I asked the question that all of you would ask: "Is it a hoax?"

"Yes," he said, "The radio man thinks it is a hoax because he cannot figure out why they would contact a nobody like him. He wonders why they did not contact the government or Einstein."

I later asked the radio man: "How do you know they have not contacted the government?" He thought this might be a reasonable assumption.

Regarding the messages we were receiving, the radio man suspected that they might be from another amateur. He noticed that the code was extremely loud and he had to turn his whole set almost completely off and the volume way down. He also noticed that the code was very fast. The radio man is not only a "ham" (amateur) operator but is also a commercially licensed operator with the Santa Fe Railroad in Arizona, and he has a reputation of being very fast on both receiving and sending. But he missed much of the messages we were receiving. He constantly asked them to slow down and they would slow down between words but not between letters. The words would come in very fast and then a long pause before the next word. He then began to realize that the messages could not be coming from another amateur.

He then thought that if they were coming from earth they might be from communists in Mexico. This was a poor idea and he did not keep this idea too long, but he thought possibly they might be communists in Mexico preparing for a landing, and when they landed we would greet them in friendship and out would come the Russians. He thought it might be a plan preliminary to an atomic bomb attack to cause panic. However, he dismissed that idea very quickly. His ham radio shack in his backyard was separated into two sections. One part was where he did repair work and the other part contained his radio set. He did technical work for the Santa Fe Railroad and also for police radios.

He noticed that if he was at his work bench, the saucer people would come in and give a preliminary warning before giving the message and when he got to the set the message would start. The warning was in the form of a couple of preliminary beats. However, if he was already at the set they never gave this preliminary warning. This gave him a very strange feeling for they seemed to know whether he was at the radio equipment or not. The messages were received in international Morse Code. One time we had radio telephone contact with the space people but the rest of the time it was radio telegraphy. The radio man decided to run some sort of a test and told them he was operating at a disadvantage because they knew who he was but he did not know who they were. He asked:

"As you have made this contact you must be interested in us. Therefore will you give us some type of assurance so that we can know that you are who you say you are?"

They replied immediately, and said: "Yes, yes. If you will get a glass we will be by Solus at high time tomorrow."

We took that to mean that if we would get a telescope they would be by the sun at noon the next day. We did not have a telescope and did not know exactly what they meant by being "by the sun." I went out the next day and looked up at the blazing sun, but of course did not see anything. However, that evening the newscast coming up from Phoenix, Arizona at 5:45 p. m. announced that a large fleet of the so called "flying saucers" had been sighted around noon that day. This could have meant something but we did not want to jump at conclusions and decided to wait until something else developed.

The next day the Los Angeles Times reported that Mount Wilson Observatory in the middle part of the previous day had observed tremendous sun spots suddenly appear on the sun. Now there is nothing unusual about sun spots on the sun, except that this was a period of declining sun spot activity. There should not be any sun spots at least not large ones, and instead of their lasting the usual two-week to thirty-day period these sun spots lasted only one day.

We do not know if there is any connection or not, or if this is just a strange coincidence. I would like to mention that I am not a technical man. One of the reasons anthropology appealed to me was that I did not have to take mathematics. It is said that the men go into anthropology because they do not have to take mathematics, and the women go into it because there are men in it! Now what I tell you as we get into more scientific terminology this evening is for you to accept or reject. I am not going to inject any of my own opinions or ideas for I am sure you are not interested in my opinions.

However, I do feel that the experiences that I have had and the experiences of others with flying saucers should be told. We were very much interested in our radio contacts and wanted to find out if it was all true. The radio man decided to run a test. He was on 40 meters and asked a question and got an immediate answer. Then very quickly he switched to 160 meters and asked another question and the answer came in promptly. The 40 meters that he was going to switch to 160 meters the man would not have had time to find him and therefore could not have heard the question and could not have answered it. That was one of the first tests he made.

Then one night a cousin of his visited him while he was in communication with another ham. He did not mention saucers to the cousin but they heard a strange buzzing sound outside. He has a fluorescent tube on the outside of his shack and when he is sending messages it flashes on and off. He asked his cousin to go outside and see if there was anything wrong. The cousin did and called to him to come outside quickly.

"You might think I'm crazy but I think that there is one of those flying saucers," he said excitedly.

Above the antenna a large orange disc was hovering but it soon took off at high speed. Then the radio man told his cousin what he had been doing in trying to establish radio contact. The radio man figured as long as they had contacted him by radio perhaps they would be willing to land in some remote area. He asked them and they replied they would be willing to land, it would just be another saucer sighting and there are hundreds of such sightings. Then the radio man made all the arrangements as to where we would go the next day to make the contact. He was to drive in one car, and we would follow him in our car.

That same evening the radio man's father-in-law came in from Tennessee. He was quite an elderly gentleman and was very senile and childish and could not keep his balance. He was really a sick man. The radio man had finished transmitting for the evening when his daughter came into the shack and told us that she had quite a problem as to what to do about the elderly gentleman. She felt they should not take him with them on the trip in which they hoped to contact the space people and she felt she could not leave him alone. If she took him on the trip and he saw something unusual he might have a heart attack and certainly she could not tell him that she was going out to contact a man from another world. Also, she was afraid that if they saw him they might not want to land.

We discussed this problem for at least an hour and we were not attempting any experiment in mental telepathy or anything like that, it never entered our minds. The receiver was on as always and all at once a message came in which said:

"Now, about the father."

Believe me I think my hair stood on end when I looked over the radio man's shoulder and saw what he was writing. The radio man turned around looking very pale and said:

"Believe me if I ever doubted, I do not now, because this is impossible but it is happening before my very eyes."

These space people told us about the old man's condition, which was verified later by a doctor. They also said there was a saline solution by the bed which was hampering the contact and asked that someone remove it and clean it up. The daughter went inside and found the solution. She came back looking very pale also. The space people seemed to know everything that went on in the ham shack and in the house. This message in connection with the elderly gentleman was the longest and I feel that it was the most significant message we received. But they said it would be all right for us to take him with us the next day. Their parting sentence was:

"Never fear the aged for they can help when they are brought back into life again."

You will all have to interpret that for yourselves, but I feel that it is very important. The next day a fourteen year old boy from next door who was staying with his uncle, a Colonel in the Air Force, came over and asked us what happened last night. The radio man thought this strange because he was on the air almost every night and the neighbors were used to this. He asked the young boy what he meant, and if he had seen anything unusual. The boy replied that he woke up, and gave the time he awakened which was the same time we were having the radio contact about the old gentleman.

He looked out from the glassed-in porch where he had been sleeping and saw a long tubular shaft of white light above the house. He could not see where it ended as it kept going straight up into space. The lower end went right down into the house and into the bedroom. The boy said he knew he was not dreaming. He was fully awake and knew what he saw. This was just another check, for no one knew what we were doing. In fact, I did not tell my father until months later but he was quite skeptical and thought we were being hoaxed. However, I have since heard from my mother and she said father finally saw a flying saucer and it was confirmed by his friend, the head of the weather bureau.

So my father is beginning to wonder too. Unfortunately we did not succeed in making our contact the next day. The radio man went on first and we were to meet him. However, in trying to follow his car we ran into a great deal of traffic and we lost him. He took a left fork in the road which we unfortunately did not see him take. We tried hard to find him but could not. When we all returned later that evening we made radio contact with the saucer people again and they said that the plans had been changed but that when all was ready we would be contacted "by a man." I did not know what they meant but that is what they said. Now I know you must wonder what all this means. It is very interesting to speak to a Venusian on the desert and to talk to a saucer by short wave radio, but really when the novelty wears off and the excitement subsides, what does it mean?

If it just means that some stray Venusian happened to drop down and talk to a man in the desert and took off again and that would be the end of it, it does not mean much. The people of the world are asking what it means. If saucers are interplanetary and they are coming here, what does it mean to us? Are they here to conquer us, are we all going to be annihilated? What does it mean and why have they come. We asked these and all manner of similar questions. One of the questions was asked by my wife as she is interested in medicine:

"You have such tremendous development in space ships, etc., have you advanced in medical science?"

They answered with just "No."

We were amazed and said: "That does not seem right. You have space ships yet you have not advanced in medical science? Why?"

The answer was: "Simple, no disease, no medical science."

They also said it was not natural for man to die in agony of cancer or other diseases, and that it is not the germs we have that cause disease. The germs are merely the scavengers and it is incorrect thinking that causes disease. We asked about the length of life on the other planets. They replied that on Mars or Venus the inhabitants live between 300 to 1500 years, and when they have learned the lessons of the planet they have been living on, and then are ready to go to the next, they merely pass out of the picture.

Believe me, this saucer business is fantastic, but even living itself is fantastic. The fact that we are alive and sitting here is fantastic. Truth is stranger than fiction and we must keep an open mind. We realize that what we know now is only a pale shadow of what we will know tomorrow. Remember the learned men in Columbus' time at the Spanish Court! Columbus was held up three years because the great scientists thought they knew all there was to know about science. They were absolutely certain that the earth was flat, but of course we know now that is not true.

The wise men should have known better, because their ancestors on this earth knew full well that the earth was round. Their ancestors also knew that other planets were inhabited. What these space people are telling us is not really new. It is only new to some of us. Remember the old saying: " There is nothing new under the sun." We asked about our atomic experiments because there is so much talk about strange weather, tornadoes, etc. They said yes, they were quite concerned about our atomic experiments.

It seems to me we should be a little concerned also. Three days after an atomic bomb was set off we had an earthquake in Turkey killing about 1,200 people. The atomic bomb blasts shake up our earth faults and contribute to some of these things.

Even our astronomers tell us that large sun spots appear on our sun, which is over 90 million miles away, when an atomic bomb is set off. If it can affect our sun so many miles away it is logical to assume that the blast contributed to the Turkey disaster. These people are concerned about our atomic bombs, but it is not our atomic bombs that are their main concern. They say that our entire solar system is moving into a new area of the universe and that cosmic ray bombardment will increase at a fast rate.

Recently a very famous American physicist announced to the scientific world that the electron count has speeded up and that the cosmic ray bombardment was increasing at a tremendous rate and that present theories would not account for it in any way. He was very alarmed. His work did not get into the newspapers. It did appear in a few scientific journals and was immediately hushed up. But, if you look in some of the back issues of Science News Letter you will find the facts. The space people told us about this even before it was announced. Another thing they told us about was the extra satellites or moons that we now have. It was only recently announced, but I happen to know that some of our people were investigating this phenomenon over two years ago. In fact our government was doing work on it two miles from us at Lowell Observatory when we had our radio contacts with space people in northern Arizona.

During this time the saucers spoke of Lowell Observatory and I know that over a million dollars worth of electronic equipment was installed on top of Mars Hill in an endeavor to locate the two satellites or artificial space stations that are now in the earth's gravitational field. This is not a secret, Frank Edwards, Washington commentator, has had it on his newscast and it has been written up in several scientific journals, etc. However, it has not been announced what these space stations are. I can state that they are not Russian space stations and they do not belong to us. They travel so rapidly that they cannot be picked up by telescope but they have been detected by electronic equipment.

The space people said that as we move into this new area of the universe there are going to be some very strange things take place on the physical, mental and spiritual planes. Peoples' minds are going to change for one thing. Also, there will be tornadoes and earthquakes. Volcanoes that have never been active in recent history will become active and erupt. Perhaps the ones in Alaska and in the Pacific that are now becoming active are perhaps part of this picture. Watch your newspapers in the small corners for the news and you can see the trend for yourself. The Ionian Island disaster was over an area in the Mediterranean where three of the earth's major fault lines converge.

Also a large explosion was felt over Seattle a couple of years ago when green fireballs exploded and caused a great reverberation throughout the Seattle area in the state of Washington. Seattle is also over an area where three of the major fault lines of the earth converge. These saucers are coming from many different places in the universe. The only thing that men on earth can accept is a physical phenomena such as a saucer or mechanical device and even then some people in the world are laughing at flying saucers. Incidentally, we were told that these ships operate in a resonating electromagnetic magnetic field. They say we have not yet discovered the fourth grade primary force of the universe, which is what they are using. It is the same force that makes a space ship out of our own planet.

ALL celestial bodies operate in a resonating electromagnetic magnetic field. The small craft have counter rotating wheels. They say that this power is to be ours also and that earth will in time be taken into the interplanetary brotherhood. Now a word about space beings. There are beings in outer space who do not eat as we do and there are those who do not have organs of speech like ours, but they use telepathy for communication. Let me tell you what these people have to say about man: They say that man is not man because he has two legs, two arms and two eyes placed in a certain position in his head or because he has come up from the anthropoid ape.

They say that man is man because he is a spiritual being, that man exists through the universe, that man as a race is an inhabitant of space, and that he takes on certain physical manifestations or vehicles on certain planets to learn certain lessons and have certain pleasure-pain experiences. We can liken our earth very simply to a school. If you had progressed beyond this earth you would not go down to the first grade and interfere with what was being taught there. The space people will not interfere with our instruction.

They say we are not going to get off this planet until we make the grade or learn the lessons this earth has to teach us. They liken it to the words of Christ: "In my Father's house there are many mansions." In space there are many planets and they say that all of them are inhabited by "life." After I had these experiences I started reading the Bible and many other things mentioned by the space people. In Hebrew it says: "the worlds were framed by the word of God." Please note that "worlds" is plural.

What about some of the astronomical theories? The science of astronomy is known as a pure and true science because it is based on mathematics. When most of us were in school, astronomers said the planet Jupiter contained deadly methane and ammonia gas. Recently they have announced through scientific journals that they were 100% wrong, Jupiter is hydrogen. If they are 100% inaccurate about one thing they are liable to be about something else. As many of you know because it has been in many of the newspapers, they have discovered that the distances to Andromeda and the other great galaxies are double the distance previously announced.

Again, they were 100% wrong. It is twice as far as they thought! This is much the situation as existed in Columbus' time. The scientists of Columbus' time were no less great because they said the earth was flat; unquestionably they represented great minds of the time. On today's mistakes are based the truth of tomorrow. These people say that all planets are inhabited to a certain extent by some type of life. They say that comets are planets in the making. That is now one of the latest astronomical theories. They are discounting the old hypothesis that we blew off from the sun. The latest theory is that planets and other celestial bodies are formed by cosmic matter accumulating in space, getting bigger and bigger like a snowball rolling down a hill.

After millions of years the comets cool off and vegetation, etc., appears and single cell life develops indigenous to that planet. Also, when the planet is ready for human life, or the classroom is all readied up, spiritual life arrives from outer space. In other words, what these people are saying is that they are your brothers and sisters and that they are not of a different creation. The only reason you and I are where we are is that we are getting certain lessons in this particular classroom.

The reason they are on Mars or Venus is because they have left our grade. They say there is no basic difference, that life came from outer space in the beginning to the planet earth. The story in Genesis of Adam and Eve is true, but is allegorical. In this case everyone of you is a "spaceman." We are all space people because we do not live underground but live on the surface of the planet so we are as much "space people" as the people on Mars. We are not space craft people for we do not travel from planet to planet, but we are space people. Very recently a professor in Finland, one of the world's foremost geographers, announced that they have discovered that practically all of the earth's bacteria that form humus is dying at a rapid rate.

It takes some nine thousand years to produce a certain humus and if it does not replenish itself it will leave in about two years. This means the possibility of famines on our earth. There is no known way of stopping this. It is continuing to die because of the increased cosmic ray bombardment. These things are absolute facts and they can be checked. The saucer people told us by radio it does not matter whether you believe who you are in contact with or not because if this thing is true it is going to happen. I have always believed what Francis Bacon said:

"Truth is the daughter of time and not the authority."

If what I say is true, it will lie on, if not it will die a very quick death and no one is going to be harmed very much. But, on the slight chance that it is true it is very important because the lives of each and every one of us are going to be changed. My life has already been completely changed by these contacts with space people. I have had to give up a large part of what I learned in school, because it cannot stand in the light of the new knowledge which is coming to us. John Robinson in England, a young astronomer, has upset many of the older astronomers by announcing that seventy miles above our earth there is a layer of pure hydrogen. In other words, if you were on Mars and you were looking through a spectroscope, you would say nothing in heaven's name could live on earth because it is hydrogen.

We know that all life, oxygen, water, vapor, etc., is found near the surface of our planet. And, as I said it has been announced that Jupiter is hydrogen; so why can not someone live on Jupiter? Another thing is that some of the astronomers seem to be such great authorities on what these other bodies are. Our so called astrophysicists say that these bodies are such and such. Recently, a well-known astronomer announced that the core of Jupiter is definitely solid. How can he know that, when our own geologists are still debating the question as to whether the core of our earth is solid or not? We do not even know the nature of our own planet under our feet. So how can we know what Jupiter is like millions upon millions of miles away? Between the spectroscope and Jupiter you have millions of miles where all kinds of cosmic debris is floating around.

That is why one time the spectroscope will get one reading from Venus and at another time will get a totally different reading with the same spectroscope. It just is not accurate. As I said before, the space people say that all planets are inhabited, and that there are twelve planets in our solar system and not nine. Of course, twelve is significant in our symbology and our historical records; such as twelve apostles, twelve months, twelve signs in the Zodiac, etc. They say there is one planet beyond Pluto and two more between Mercury and the sun. One of these has already been seen in transit in the late eighteen hundreds across the sun's surface and was named Vulcan, but it was not accepted by most of the scientific world. The contacts that we had were mostly with Mars, Venus, Jupiter and Saturn. They say that Saturn is the tribunal or headquarters of our solar system.

There have been many debates as to whether the saucerians are etheric. Are they from other worlds, other dimensions, are they invisible or are they discarnate spirits? In other words, by dying do we merely pass into another dimension, another world? Is that what the saucer beings are? Are they beings like ourselves in a three dimensional world on another planet such as Mars or even in another system? All of these concepts are apparently accurate to a certain degree. Saucers are coming from many different places; from our own solar system, from other solar systems which are in our own dimension and they are also coming from higher dimensions.

They claim that at the present time there are fifty-one solar systems in the confederation and that they have over three and one-half million space craft surrounding our planet at the present time. They have been following out a definite plan. They say that they have agents throughout the earth. These fall into several groups. They say there was an influx of people from other worlds by space craft transportation in the eighteen hundreds. The microfilm libraries in various newspaper morgues tell of enormous spaceships seen in our atmosphere at this period.

Another group consists of about ten million people not of earth origin now on the surface of our planet. About six million of these are now in the United States. This group did not just now step off from saucers. They are here through the reincarnation cycle, and starting about 1947 the saucer beings began a program of waking up these people to the fact that they lived originally on other planets. The saucers also now land their own people here to perform certain definite jobs. These space people do not live among us permanently. They are only here for short periods.

They also say that the reason we on earth have progressed more in the last fifty years than we had in the last ten thousand years is because of this type of assistance coming from outer space. They have further said that certain people will be taken from our earth to other planets. However, there will be those who will not be taken for the simple reason that they themselves are not perfect and some people on earth if taken to their planet might incorrectly influence the minds of some of their own people. However, some people are being taken now and they will be instructed and returned here to be used as teachers.

I want to make it very clear that I am not representing any church or any particular group and my opinions are not important; I can only repeat what was said by the space people. They say life is eternal and that Christ is in charge of the planet earth. The saucer people are the "hosts" that were prophesied about as coming to earth proceeding the Second Coming of Christ. They say it is true that Christ will return and that there will be a judgment day. There will also be earthquakes, etc.

Certain souls have progressed to a certain stage where the new earth will be for them; all others who have not reached this stage of growth will go elsewhere. They say only the good will remain on earth, that is those of a certain evolvement. As for the judgment day, the "judgment" is merely our own development. Some will be able to live in the new higher vibration, and some will not. All will, however, land in the "school" best suited for their growth. There is now a tremendous interest in our planet from outer space. These people claim they are not gods, they are only a little bit ahead of us and they still make plenty of mistakes. They figured that we would discover nuclear energy about 1950 but because of our second world war and the speed-up in technical advances this came about in the 40's.

They said they knew our whole system was passing into a new area of the universe and that certain things had to be done because certain conditions will not exist on earth in the new vibratory rate. They are not going to interfere in the sense of coming down and stopping what we are learning in this classroom. Now some of us wonder why God himself in all his mercy does not or has not stopped wars on this earth. Or we wonder why the space people, if they are so grand and powerful - why they do not stop wars. It is because there are certain souls that need to experience wars, and after they are blown up about twenty thousand times the soul finally realizes that it is all a little ridiculous.

These people do not like to see war, they do not like to see the cream of our youth destroyed in wars, and much of our good attainment destroyed. But at the same time they do not look upon death as we do. They claim that life is eternal and therefore if you leave one physical vehicle it does not matter very much because you live forever anyway. When they see our boys die on the battlefield they realize it is not death. Nevertheless we are told that the New Age will eventually see the end of all wars on this planet forever. They also say that we are the only warring planet in this section of the universe.

We are not the only planet that has wars, but in this section of the universe we are the only warring planet. To give you an example they said they know of a system where the people have just invented the wheel and have an axle and found out that if they put beeswax on the axle it would not wear out so quickly. So there are places where men are still running around with clubs, and there are planets that are just cooling off. It is a continual process and I might add that the whole thing is a circular affair.

We are heading toward perfection but we are the planet of lowest development in this section of the universe. In other words, we thought we were so grand but we are not — we seem to be more like the garbage can! During my lecture in Cincinnati I referred to our earth as the "garbage can" of our system. One woman said she could believe of this but that she just could not believe that any thing in all creation could have anything superior to what the United States has! Well, that is very nice and I am proud that I am a United States citizen and I am proud of our attainments and developments but after all we have to face the facts. Anyway she did not like the garbage can idea! Another woman asked me what they said about Hell. I told her their idea was this: We are in it right now!

One time we told the Venusians that their world sounded like heaven. They said we must not say that because they are still very crude, and that they know of a planet which is six trillion years ahead of them. They said that man does not always take the form that we know now. Believe me this is getting very fantastic, but I give it because it was what we were told. They said that they know of worlds, although they cannot comprehend them, where man is geometric in form. Imagine, if you can, a cube or a triangle going along together! It is just beyond our comprehension. As the Bible says:

"Eye has not seen or ear has not heard what the Father has in store for us."

These people say that this is true. On this planet we have a certain physical form. We as spiritual beings took this form in order to learn the lessons that this particular planet has to offer. Major fault lines cover the earth. When the government decided where to perform our atomic experiences they picked a place where the least amount of people would have to be moved, and the southwest was decided upon in New Mexico. Unfortunately, these experiments were set off right over two of our major fault lines.

When the big atomic test was made in the Pacific around March 25, about a day later there occurred some terrific earthquakes in the Hawaiian Islands. The atomic bombs are not causing the strange conditions but they are accentuating an already dangerous situation and our lines of weakness are under more strain and stress now because of the atomic bomb experiments. If you find a small crack in the ground and you stomp around on it you may weaken it and the whole thing may give away. Yes, there will be catastrophes. In fact they have already started. Earthquakes will increase, certain lands will go under. The polar caps are melting at a very fast rate which is why there were icebergs seen off Florida recently. Also avalanches occurred in Europe which buried entire villages. The snow is melting very fast. Ice flows occurred in the northern European harbors not many months ago, which clogged the harbors so that ships could not get in or out.

These people say the, world is not coming to an end. The world will not end. It is only that the true Golden Age which we once knew upon earth will return — the Golden Age that all historians talk about, when man had the ability to speak with angels. Disease will no longer exist. War will no longer plague us. They also assure us that life is

27

eternal. They say they believe in a Creator, the same God as we do but they also said that:

"You worship by word and not by deed."

May I say that when these people speak they never speak in a derogatory way against any nation, race or church. When they speak of us they speak of us as a totality — or the people of earth. They are interested in everyone in the world. Some people suggest that religion be left out of this subject. But how can you leave religion out of it. It is connected. Many people will say that I sound like a Mormon, an Oaspian, a Christian Scientist or some other kind of religionist, and that many of the things I say are things they have learned in their church. All of the religions have some of the truth. These people told us that God provided, but that man divided.

We are always dividing. That is why we have so many churches and so many philosophies. For a long time science has been on the left and religion on the far right, but more and more through the years they have been coming together. How can truth contradict truth? There is no religion higher than truth and if science has some of that truth and religion has some of the same truth, that truth cannot contradict itself. I feel that the scientist must recognize the truth of religion, and the religionist must recognize the truth of science. Perhaps there will have to be a big explosion to fuse them together in our minds. But in the minds of the space people they are already one. In fact they have always been one, because truth will not contradict truth wherever it is found.

They also told us that under the new cosmic ray bombardment all falsity and hoaxes will pass away. We will not have to wonder, is this or that true. We will know! This is one of the mental changes that will come about. Watch your newspapers and you will see many things being shown up for what they are. You can call it the true light coming from Aquarius, you can call it a new vibration, or a new density, or you can call it a new dimension or the New Golden Age. In the fall of last year we left the old third density and we are no longer in it. We are in the transitional stage or in the beginning of a new dimension or new density right now. As the change is coming slowly we do not notice it too much. Many people say we are going from Pisces to Aquarius.

These space people are here merely to help us, and to usher us into this new dimension — usher us into this New Age. Regardless of what we do there is a New Age coming. People are wondering what is going to happen in the future. The space beings said they would not interfere with our education, but there was a qualification to this. This may seem like a contradiction but I will try to make it clear. They will eventually interfere if we decide upon atomic war. If we decide on a peaceful "one-world" they will land and assist us into the New Age on earth. If we decide on aggressive war they will let the war go on a certain length of time because there are certain souls on earth that must have this lesson, and then they will interfere for our planet must not be destroyed, nor the peaceful and constructive minded inhabitants. At one time they said:

"We are here to conquer earth, but conquer the earth with love."

Now the big question is when is all this going to take place. We asked this question repeatedly.

Our radio messages said many times: "Very soon — soon — soon."

We replied: "Maybe 10,000 years to you is soon. What do you mean by soon?"

They answered: "When we say soon, we mean soon as you think of soon!"

Impatient as we are that must be pretty quick! Whether you believe what I have told you or not does not matter. But keep your eyes on the skies. Keep an open mind and look into this thing for yourselves and give it some serious attention. We are actually entering a New Age on this earth! I have enjoyed talking to you very much and would like to know each and everyone of you. Thank you!

1 PROLOGUE

This documentary report on communication with space craft in the Earth's atmosphere covers the period from 2 August 1952 until February 1953.

Communication was also established with several planets in our own Solar System and with space craft in our atmosphere from other Solar Systems.

For the most part, all messages were received in International Morse Code through radiotelegraphy. There was one instance, where radiotelephony was employed by the space craft intelligences.

The egotistical idea that our puny Earth is the hub of the universe should have died out with Ptolemaic or Earth-centre theory. If we believe in Infinity then there must be billions upon billions of earths and solar systems. It can be concluded by reason alone that other planets, many exceeding this Earth in magnitude, are not vacant masses, created only to be borne along and revolve around the Sun, and shine just for the pleasure of men on Earth. The Creator has created the Universe for no other end than that the human race may exist. Wherever there is an earth, there are or will be men.

Science knows that there are at least 1,000,000 other planetary systems in our own Milky Way Galaxy. A lot of room for a lot of people. Spectroscopic analysis, and our own misconceptions and conceit are the only factors against life on other worlds. We take intense delight in thinking of ourselves as Lords of Creation and in some cases, even deny the Creator Himself. Our egotism chokes and blinds us to reality and we deny what we know in our heart to be true. The spectroscope is inaccurate and this fact has been known and proven many times. The great observatories of our world, dedicated to scientific truth know that the other planets are inhabited by men and they know what the flying saucers are, too!

We are not the only ones who have been fortunate enough to make contact with the saucer intelligences. There are many other devoted and sincere workers throughout the world who are receiving messages by radiotelegraphy and other methods. The valuable information in their possession is almost identical with ours in every case.

These messages constitute a warning to men on the planet of the third orbit or Earth. There isn't any threat of invasion; but as a father warns a child of danger, these people who are wiser than we, are telling us we have already done untold damage to our world through the use of Atomic Energy. Perhaps it would be more accurate to say, the misuse of that energy. The space craft intelligences know exactly what our insane experimentation has done in the past and they know the prevailing conditions on earth at this time.

Look at the increase in tidal waves, earthquakes, volcanic eruptions, plane crashes, sea disasters, the strange world-wide weather, and the recent floods in Great Britain, Belgium and the Netherlands. We have but to look about us and we immediately know what we have done.

It is realized that many will not believe this report and will therefore reject it. But, there will be many more who will believe and who will accept its message and attempt to warn the world. We are not trying to prove anything to anyone. We have received this information from a great and noble people, and it is our duty **to** give it to our fellowman in truth.

Read the following account with an open mind. Think about it seriously, for it is a message in a time of world unrest.

This work is dedicated to the Brotherhood of Man in answer to the desperate need of a stricken world. In profound humility we thank those who have come a great distance to aid us at this time. Those who desire and seek truth have called this work forth, and for them it was recorded.

GEORGE HUNT WILLIAMSON

Prescott, Arizona

15 February 1953

What read we here?—Th' existence of a God?

Yes; and of other beings, Man above!

Native of aether! sons of higher climes!

'Tis thus the skies

Inform its of superiors numberless,

As much in excellence above mankind,

As above earth, in magnitude, the spheres.

—Old Poem

2 OTHER VOICES

Ancient records show beyond the shadow of a doubt that the saucers have been here for centuries. When radio was developed on the Earth, things began to happen.

The first report was made by the father of wireless himself, Marconi. In September 1921, J. C. H. MacBeth, London manager of the Marconi Wireless Telegraph Company arrived in New York and told astonished reporters that Marconi believed he had intercepted messages from Mars or some point in outer space. The signals, MacBeth said, had been received while Marconi was on his yacht in the Mediterranean conducting atmospheric experiments with wireless. Magnetic wave lengths high in the meter band had been picked up, although the maximum length of Earth produced waves at that time was 14,000 meters. The theory that the waves were produced by electrical disturbances was disproved by the regularity of the impulses. Although the impulses apparently consisted of a code, the only signal similar to Earth codes was one resembling the letter V in the Marconi code.

Marconi's experiment is interesting because he, too, received the strange V. In almost all of the radio contacts made by Mr. R, this letter was frequently given.

In the following years, as radio was developed, a number of interesting discoveries were made. L. W. Chubb, director of research for the Westinghouse Electric Company, in announcing the perfection of beam radio transmission, stated that if communications with Mars was ever established, it would have to be with ultra short waves directed like a beam of light in order to penetrate the atmospheric layers above the Earth's surface. Ultra-short waves are the nearest approach of radio waves to regular light waves. The Heaviside-Kennelly Layer is about seventy miles above the surface. At double that height is the Appleton Layer. These are layers of ionized gas that reflect radio waves. The Heaviside-Kennelly Layer reflects medium waves and the Appleton Layer the short waves. Beam transmission experiments, however, were made by the Danish expert, Hals, and two Scandinavian scientists, Stormer and Peterson, and they found that certain short waves penetrate both layers and travel far out into space.

Their signal echoes arrived from three to thirty seconds after transmission. Since the velocity of radio waves is the same as light, 186,000 miles per second (now known to be faster), it was obvious that the "layers" or bodies that reflected these signals were located at from 280,000 to 2,800,000 miles from the Earth. Apparently even these "layers" far out into space could be penetrated by a beamed wave approaching a regular light wave which passes through all ionized barriers.

Plans for a regular light beam signal were made by Harry Price, director of the National Laboratory of Psychical Research in London in 1930, but the project was abandoned due to insufficient funds. The site selected was the summit of Jungfraujoch in the Bernese Oberland, 11,000 feet above sea level. Ten tons of magnesium was to be ignited in oxygen in the focus of reflectors, and the beam directed on the snowfields of the Martian pole. This colossal flare, it was believed, would certainly bring a response if there were intelligent beings on the mystery planet.

On the night of 22 August 1924, the planet Mars approached to within thirty-four and a half million miles of the Earth. Radio silence prevailed from the broadcasting stations and scientists listened for a possible message from across space. Station WOR at Newark, New Jersey, was the first listening post to report. Other stations followed. And in Washington, DC, a photographic film record of the impulses was being made which has never been understood.

Plans for the experiment had been carefully laid. Dr. David Todd, Professor Emeritus of Astronomy at Amherst College, was the organizer of the international "listening in" test. At Dr. Todd's suggestion the United States Government, through channels of diplomacy, requested that all countries with high power transmitters silence their stations for five minutes every hour from 11:50 p.m., 21 August to 11:50 p.m., 23 August. C. Francis Jenkins, of Washington, D C, had only recently invented a radio photo message continuous recording machine, and he was asked by Dr. Todd to take a record of any signals received during the experiment.

The recording device was attached to a receiving set adjusted to a wave length of 6,000 meters. Incoming signals caused flashes of light which were printed on the film by an instrument passing over its surface from side to side. The film was in the form of a roll tape, thirty feet long and six inches wide, and it was slowly unwound under the instrument and light bulb which responded to the transmitted sounds.

The Jenkins device was in operation for a period of about thirty hours during all moments of silence while Mars was closest to the Earth. Then the film was developed, and on 27 August, the astonished experimenters called in newspaper reporters. The film disclosed in black on white a fairly regular arrangement of dots and dashes along one side, but on the other side, at almost evenly spaced intervals, were curiously jumbled groups each taking the form of a crudely drawn human face. The inventor did not think that Mars was the cause of the phenomenon, but he said, "The film shows a repetition at intervals of about a half-hour of what appears to be a man's face, and it's a freak which we can't explain."

Although admitting that he was at a loss to explain its significance, Dr. Todd took a more serious view. He said, "We now have a permanent record which can be studied, and who knows until we have studied it, just what these signals may have been?" Army code experts worked on the film for some weeks without reaching any decisions, and a copy of the film was given to the radio division of the Bureau of Standards. The film is there today, and it is claimed it has never been understood.

It seems the significance of the human face is obvious, taking for granted it did come from somewhere in outer space. A crudely drawn human face would be a "calling card" of the human race anywhere!

The film had only deepened the mystery of the dots and dashes reported heard by widely separated operators of powerful stations. News dispatches of 23 August announced that R. L Potelle, chief engineer of Station WOR, Newark, New Jersey, between 7:30 and 10:00 p.m. on the preceding evening, received a series of dots and dashes that belonged neither to the Morse nor Continental codes. The signals were steadily repeated. After hours of study, the engineer decided that the word being transmitted was EUNZA. The word has no meaning in the languages of earth.

The word EUNZA reminds us again of our radio experiments. You will note later that we received the letters E U. It is possible that there is some connection? Is our E U really just a part of EUNZA?

An attempt to contact Mars by radio was made in October 1928, by Mansfield Robinson, a London lawyer, through the Rugby station in England. The message was sent on an 18,700 meter wave length, and it was hoped that some sort of response might be heard. A few minutes after Robinson's message went out through space, Professor A. M. Low, the famous English scientist who was listening in, received a series of signals on his radio. He said: "It was a mysterious message, but it is hardly likely that it could have come from Mars. However, I must confess that I do not know who sent it. It was a series of dots and dashes."

Here was a group attempting radio contact with Mars, yet when they received a reply they refused to accept the obvious! That is as stupid as deliberately going to the telephone, dialing a certain number, and when the party answers, saying to him: "I can't understand you, but you couldn't be my party anyway."

Strange things were happening amongst the amateur radio men, too. In July of 1950, Byron Goodman (W 1 DX), Assistant Technical Editor of QST (official organ of the American Radio Relay League, Inc. and the International Amateur Radio Union), wrote an article entitled, "The Loneliest Ham in the World." This article appeared in QST (Volume xxxiv, No. 7).

Mr. Goodman's strange account and experience follows:

It was a good convention, although the rains may have held down the attendance a little. At the DX meeting I mentioned how at League Headquarters we often enjoy the confidences of foreign hams who are forced to operate under cover, and how these operators in the less "enlightened" countries really have a tough time of it. It just happens to be one of the interesting sidelights to working at the League, and I've told about it lots of times, without giving away any calls, of course.

The wind-up banquet was over early, and I figured it was a good chance to catch up on my sleep. But just as I got to my room the phone rang, and a voice at the other end asked if he could come up and talk a little DX. Well, no matter how tired you are you don't pass up something like that, so I told him, "Sure. Come on up."

I'd put my guest in his 50's, but of course you never know. He told me his call, which didn't ring any bells, and his name.

He took his with soda, and then announced, "Boy, I've worked more DX than anyone else in the world."

Oh, brother! I thought. A crackpot. I know W_1FH and a few of the others, and this guy wasn't one of them.

"I don't follow you, Mike," I said. "W_1FH has the most confirmed, and there are a few others right on his tail. How many have you got?"

"If you mean countries," he said. "I don't have any. I'm talking about *real* DX. I have to tell someone or I'll bust. I figure I can talk to you because you know how to keep a confidence."

"Oh, you can trust me," I said, knowing I had about forty pounds and a few years on him. And I was closer to the door. "What do you call *real* DX?"

He sipped his drink and looked straight at me. He didn't look like a nut. His eyes were clear without the glitter, and he wasn't a nervous type. "Planets," he said quietly. "I've worked four of them."

My first reaction was to gag it and ask if he had the QSLs, but then I thought better of it. "What makes you think I'll believe that, or even think it's funny?" I asked.

"Look, it's early," he replied. "Come on out to the shack and I'll show you. The Eastern train goes out at 9 a.m., and I'll bring you back before midnight. You'll get your beauty sleep."

I'm a sucker for any new angle, so I went. He briefed me while I watched his Buick's headlights take us through town and out the highway. "I got interested in 5 meters when hams were debasing tubes to get on 20," he said. "That's a long time ago, and I hadn't had my ticket very long. There wasn't a soul around here on 5, but I didn't know enough to realize there weren't a lot of fellows on across the country. After all, QST reported activity there."

"That was before my time," I explained. "Don't blame me."

"I called CQ on 5 every night every ten minutes for I don't know how long," he continued. "Then one night, as I turned around after my second or third CQ, I heard someone calling me. I was so shaky going back I almost pulled the key off the table. The signal signed MA₁A but I never gave it a thought.'"

It was someone I could work, and that was good enough for me. I gave him a signal report and signed over. He didn't come back! I was frantic! Here he was, the first station I'd ever raised, and I lost him! Then, fully seven or eight minutes later, I ran across his signal acknowledging my report and telling me I was very weak. He wasn't weak at all, and before we were through he had told me how to build a decent antenna, although I had a little trouble at times understanding his English. It was a screwy kind of skywire, like nothing in the books then or now. We made a schedule for the next night, and during the day I built the antenna. When schedule time came I called with a lot of confidence, but no answer. Then, after a lapse of about seven or eight minutes I heard him! This time we chewed the fat for five hours, always with the delay in his comeback. What he told me that night left me in a daze. He said he was on Mars! They had heard me calling QC every night, and practicing the code in between, and they had managed to dope out the language from what I had sent all those months. It's true I had been amusing myself by practicing the code on the air-sending a page at a time from *QST* or Scientific American—but I didn't see how they could figure out the whole language from that. It turned out that they hadn't really, but after a few weeks of schedules and a lot of questions MA₁A knew the language as well as I did. From the first he told me that if I mentioned this to anyone else our schedule would stop, so I didn't tell a soul.

I kept looking for an angle. All I could figure was a big leg-pulling deal, so I rode along. "When was all this?" I asked.

"Oh, it started back in the 20's," Mike replied. "Since then we've moved higher in frequency, and he's told me how to build in secrecy systems so no one will ever get on to us. I can't tell you the details, but we never stay on the same frequency long enough for anyone to spot us. We swish through the 2-metre band hundreds of times an hour, but nothing would ever tag us except a TV receiver in that range."

"And you've been keeping this schedule ever since?" I asked.

"That and a few more. When we first started, MA₁A asked a lot of questions, and I noticed that when I told him about our aeroplanes and submarines and guns he wasn't much interested. But since the war I have to go through all the magazines and papers for any dope on jet planes and rockets and atomic energy, because he asks a lot of questions about what we're doing with them. Ever since he told me how to build a real antenna and a good station, we've had a solid circuit. He and his friends are smart ones, all right. The things they tell me always work, and it's all stuff that hasn't been in *QST* or even the I. R. E. Proceedings. As he helped me improve my rig, he started hooking me up with some of the other planets."

This is really getting thick, I thought.

"Apparently these guys or things on Mars taught the earth language, at least my version of it, to the other planets, and told how to get in touch with me. I figured the whole thing might be a hoax, so I read up on astronomy and darned if everything didn't check. Our dates were made only for times the other planets were visible on this side of the world, and the delay time always checked out on the button. The toughest place to get to was Jupiter, and I finally had to raise my peak power to 200 kilowatts before I could get through, although I'd been hearing them for weeks."

What do you mean, "peak power," I asked. "Are you using pulse?"

"Sure," Mike replied. "It's the only way I can get through and not have tubes that would look suspicious, just in case the law ever comes around. I put that in back in 1932, when I first worked Venus. Anyway, it's part of our secrecy system."

"How about phone? Didn't you try it so you can hear what their voices sound like?"

"I suggested it," said Mike. "But they said 'No.' Code was good enough for all they needed, they claimed. I figured they didn't want to tip me off, in case they don't have voices and would have to create artificial ones."

It sounded reasonable enough, but I wasn't buying any until I saw it. Just then Mike turned off the highway onto a dirt road, and we finally ended up in a small house. In the moonlight I could see a lot of masts.

"My antenna is made of wires strung from those poles," Mike explained. "I change the directivity by phasing from the shack, and I explain to the few hams who have wandered by that it's an experimental 40-metre beam. I'm never on 40, they don't hear me, and they lose interest."

Inside the shack the stuff looked real good. I didn't see anything that looked like unusual techniques, though, and I wondered out loud about the secret stuff. Mike smiled and explained that the place had to look something like a ham station—the secret gear was hidden away and I was wasting my time snooping.

"When's your next date?" I asked.

"Tomorrow night," Mike replied. "But we can interrogate the band if you want, just in case someone's on." He warmed up the rig a few minutes and then threw a switch. The lights dimmed a bit and I heard a few transformers groan. A pip appeared on the panoramic and Mike centered it. He sat down at the table and worked the guy on the bug. The call was MM_1F but I wasn't impressed, because a lot of jokers with queer calls have sucked me in during the past decade or two, and I believe them when I get a QSL. Mike and MM_1F exchanged reports and then chewed the fat about an ionosphere storm that was due, working fast break-in. MM_1F could have been a ZL for all the difference it would have made in the procedure. I had to admire his fist, though it sounded just like tape. Then it dawned on me that the whole thing was a rib! There was no delay in the comeback! Some of the local boys must have planned the whole thing to make a monkey out of the New Englander. But the op at the other end had forgotten to allow some lag time! Pretty good, I thought, but they slipped up after all the elaborate built-up. I'll just play along.

Mike signed off, there were no more pips on the screen, and he shut down and made a pot of coffee. We chewed about receiver sensitivity, pulse techniques, beam antennas, and the usual. I had to hand it to him—he knew all the answers. Occasionally I would get around to his rig, but he would brush me off on the tough questions with the excuse that they involved the secret stuff. On the way back to the hotel it was much the same deal, but he did give me a few ideas I'm going to try. That one about compound feedback has possibilities.

Mike made me promise I wouldn't tell a soul about his work, declined a nightcap, and then I gave him the business. "By the way, Mike," I asked, "why wasn't there any delay on that planet MM_1F you worked!"

"Oh, that was no planet," Mike replied. "That was a mobile station, a space ship practically in our atmosphere. There are quite a few around these days, scouting the earth. Look me up when you're out this way again." He drove off before I had a chance to tell him I had the whole thing figured.

But have I? I just read about two airline pilots who have *seen* the darned things!

There are several things about Mike's experience that tic-in with our own experiments. First of all, he said that the transmission from Mars, etc., was never "weak." The signals we received were never "weak" either. He said that the language they used was strange. Could it be they spelled phonetically as they did with us? He also said that Jupiter was the most difficult planet to contact. You will note later our own radio records, and know that we had the same experience. They wouldn't use radiotelephony with Mike, and they only used it once with us.

Yes, the saucers have been here for centuries, and the moment we developed our crude radio communication, they utilized that also.

3 WILLIAMSON: HIS STORY

It was a rainy afternoon in mid-summer on the shores of Spirit Bear Lake. This was the northern land of Minnesota, USA. It had always been the same, I mused, as I stretched out on my cabin cot to read. The Redman, the Norseman, the Whiteman; they had all been captivated by the 'Land of the Sky-Blue Water.' Evidence is on every hand to prove that they all were acquainted with this country of mounds, mooring-stones and logging camps.

It was in 1951 and I was doing anthropological field-work amongst the Chippewa Indians. I had already accumulated many legends of these wonderful Woodland people. Woven into their age-old stories of 'Hairy-Faced Men,' 'Gee-By's' (Ghosts), and Nanabozho, were countless tales of the 'Gin-Gwin' or that which shakes the Earth. These 'Earth-Rumblers' might also be known as `Flying Wheels' or `Flying Boats.'

The venerable old Chippewa men still tell of the sacred 'Little People' in a whisper. These highly intelligent little men were said to have appeared in ancient times to the people of the Chippewa nation. While they were with the Indians they taught them better ways of living. If you ask the Indian why these wise beings are no longer seen, they will tell you, 'They don't come around much any more since the white man came.'

After many months of hearing and recording these legends, I still never associated them in any way with the saucer phenomena that was puzzling the entire world.

So, on this rainy afternoon, I began to read the pocketbook edition of Donald Keyhoe's, *The Flying Saucers Are Real.* Once started, I couldn't put it down until I had finished it. It continued to rain and I continued to read. He spoke of that day in Tucson, Arizona when thousands of people looked up to see 'something' in the sky. I had been in Tucson when all of this happened and I had seen that something myself. Now facts began to snap into place in my mind. I had always believed that this Earth must certainly not be the only inhabited world in the entire universe. Why would the Creator place man, his crowning achievement on one, rather small, insignificant planet? After all, there must be many planets and solar systems in outer space. Why would any earth be created to spin around eternally void of life; to fulfill its mission as a noxious ball of poisonous gas full of methane and ammonia? I felt that other worlds were created for one purpose only—to be the abode of Man!

Yes, I could accept Keyhoe's conclusion that the flying saucers were interplanetary in origin. They could be from planets in our own solar system, or they could even be from other solar systems. And then I seemed to hear uproarious laughter because I felt that the men of other worlds must think it humorous indeed that men of Earth on their little speck believe that the entire universe was created just for them. These men must also feel somewhat sad at the same time because such ignorance abounds.

I now collected my legends and so-called myths in a more serious manner. Where before I had not deliberately looked for saucer stories, I now intentionally dug them out. At the Chippewa rice camps, the Squaw Dances, the country grocery store and in the fishing boats, we talked saucers—the Redman and I.

Soon I discovered that the saucers existed in the tales of almost all the American Indian tribes and even in the legends of so-called primitive people all over the world! There were the 'Flying Boats' of ancient India and the Orient. The 'Flying Boats' and the 'Havmusuvs' of the Paiutes and Navajos in the American Southwest. The 'Little Wise People' of the Sioux, Mandan, Cherokee and many other tribes. The strange, almost forgotten tales of Poseid (Atlantis), Lemuria, Mu, and Pan the Lost Continents where men had the knowledge of 'Flying Ships.' And in the Holy Bible itself I found an obvious reference to saucers in the Old Testament, Book of the Prophet Ezekiel, Chapter 1.

I returned to Arizona in the spring of 1952 and decided to continue my research, hoping to find some of the answers, at least, to the age-old mystery of the saucers and wheels. What were they? Where did they come from? What—if anything—was inside? What were they here for? I knew that somewhere there were answers to these and other questions. I wanted to find out.

I joined my wife in Prescott, Arizona. She had been conducting her own research in anthropology near Tucson, Arizona, and had her own across many strange tales also. We then began to read everything that had ever been published on the saucer phenomena. Keyhoe, Heard, Scully, Arnold, Palmer, and others.

During the summer months the saucers were headlined again and again. This time they were seen over the Washington Capitol mad were even picked-up on radarscopes.

One evening in late summer, Mr. and Mrs. Alfred C. Bailey of Winslow, Arizona, came to visit with my wife and I in Prescott. I had corresponded with Al and Betty and knew them to be people interested in ancient history, philosophy, and anthropology. Al was employed by the Santa Fe Railways Company, but antiquities had always fascinated him and he made quite a hobby of it.

We discussed my research work in the Northern United States and what I had discovered while there. Inevitably, the conversation got around to saucers. Neither the Baileys nor my wife and I were absolutely certain as to what they might be. We did know, however, that the so-called official statements regarding them were very absurd and only confused the entire matter. A noted South American scientist claimed they were corpuscles passing over the retina of the eye. Another said they were seeking cotton puff balls floating in the New Mexico skies from Texas. Others said they were flying hubcaps, tow-targets, weather instruments, temperature inversion, etc.

We both had always believed that other worlds must be inhabited. Even most astronomers agree on that point. So, we decided that if the saucers were piloted by intelligent beings, they must be wiser than we. They must be, for they have developed space craft and we have not. Therefore, they would be able to understand our language by now and our code systems as well. This seems difficult for most people to understand. They ask, 'But how can the "saucerians" speak English?' Let me say it is not impossible by any means. We speak a language, don't we? And we learned it as children by hearing it spoken. As we get older it is harder for us to learn a language but we can learn it, nevertheless. Are we to limit them to our own intelligence? We have already proven that they are much wiser than we. But let us say for a moment that they are only as intelligent as we are (perish the thought). They then could learn our language in about six months by merely listening to it. Anthropology can explain this fact easily.

If one goes into a foreign land and wishes to learn the language of that land, he finds someone who is bilingual to teach him. However, if no one there understands him and he doesn't understand them, he has no alternative but to listen to them day in and day out. After about six months (this varies with different individuals, of course) he will begin to know what they are talking about. Sometime later he will learn to speak the language himself. So, you see, it is not too difficult to understand how they can speak our languages or know our code systems.

If there were intelligent beings in those saucers they must be observing our world—listening to everything we say by monitoring our radio broadcasts. We wondered what their purpose in coming to Earth was. We didn't think it conceivable that with countless planets in space they would desire our beloved Earth that we have contaminated for so many centuries. Besides, if they have been coming here for so long, why didn't they invade and conquer us when we were quite harmless with our bow and arrow playthings? Certainly they wouldn't wait until we had developed atomic weapons of war! Therefore, we knew that they had not traversed millions of miles of space for conquest.

We spent the rest of our evening together in Prescott enjoying a line supper in town and entertaining ourselves with certain games and parlour tricks. One amusing pastime known to many families as a diverting trick is automatic writing. We thought it would be fun to try it. We had heard that the idea was for one or two people to hold a pencil over a sheet of paper and then see if it would write some sort of a message. Although there are some who seriously consider the writing obtained in this manner to be genuine spirit communication, we never had such thoughts in our minds. We were just doing what many people will do in their own parlour for an evening's entertainment. In truth, since our dinner, we had just about forgotten the elusive saucers, and now were having a good time. What we did not know was the people of other worlds were watching and waiting f or a sign of receptivity on the part of their brothers on Earth, standing by and ready with their superior equipment to contact any and all who sought the answer to their presence in the skies of Earth. Little did we know what we had started with our simple little amusement. It was to change our entire life!

If what we were receiving through automatic writing was true, then there would be answers to many questions. Had we, through our intense desire to know more about the saucers, actually contacted the intelligence behind them? It didn't seem at all possible, but how could we be sure?

For centuries man on Earth has pondered the debatable question: Is there life on other worlds? If so, and this life is human, are there homes and cities where men live, love and work? We looked up into black space, pin-pointed with millions of these worlds, and wondered.

4 ALFRED C. BAILEY: HIS STORY

During my school years, and for reasons not known or understood, I was at variance with my instructors and textbooks. I had a strong tendency to argue and disbelieve both the teachers and their many theories that they taught as 'fact.'

As I look back now, throughout my entire life, I can see where man-made ideas and opinions have been relegated to the back of my mind. However, it was always easy for me to accept ideas of a universal nature, and to reject or disregard effect ideas that were being taught.

Perhaps during my grade school years this unknown factor was the thing that made my life so hard. After entering high school I found it much easier to get along even if I did not completely agree with my instructors.

In 1933 I met Dr. F. E. Dewart, a chiropractor, of Peru, Indiana. Until this time my concept of chiropractic was as hazy and biased as most young people's. Dr. Dewart explained to me in concise and simple language the theory of his profession. It was so natural and reasonable that it immediately intrigued me. From his simple explanation of how and why the human body worked I decided to study this science.

In the fall of 1933 I entered the Palmer School of Chiropractic. I did not complete the prescribed course of study, but did learn enough of it to know that certain Universal Laws as taught there apply to almost every phase of scientific research and to life itself.

The philosophy is based upon the understanding and the acceptance of the existence of a Universal Intelligence. It starts with that great universal principle of cause. As long as that part of their philosophy, upon which their science is based, is kept in mind, they or anyone else following a line of scientific research cannot be far wrong.

Any scientific study based on that great principle of the universe studying effects proceeding from cause instead of trying to arrive at causes by studying effects cannot but be well based in fact instead of theory.

Even though I did not finish my chiropractic study and failed to enter practice, I am glad that I attended their school. I learned to understand the Laws of the Universe a little more. Six or seven years ago I broke with a dogmatic religion. From that time until now I have in no way felt lost but learned that no religion offered all the necessary answers to the universe. At least, none of them answered my inner-most feelings.

I liked the American Southwest. It had an exceptional climate and good employment was to be had in my field of railroading. Winslow, Arizona, is a typical railroad town. I have worked for the Santa Fe Railway Company for many years, and now serve them as a conductor.

Although I had little formal education in science, I read many books on various subjects. Several of these books spoke of the flying saucers. Soon I began to believe that these strange sky objects might be space craft from other inhabited planets. The writings of many others then began to fill a gap in my mind to help me understand our universal belonging.

Many of my friends and co-workers in the past few years have been surprised by my positive statements that these saucers were space ships or observation craft from larger space ships. Since I had never placed much reliance on scientific pronouncements of the uninhabitable nature of the planets in our solar system, it seemed only proper and reasonable that they were visitors from neighbouring planets.

Everything went along in this manner for several years. I was in no way a flying saucer fanatic. I had accepted them for what many people now know them to be.

One day last summer (1952), we received a letter from George H. Williamson, an anthropologist living in Prescott, Arizona. He knew our mutual interest and said that if we were ever in Prescott we should come to see him and his wife. This letter was ignored for almost two months. Then, one day, we decided to take the time to make the somewhat long drive through Flagstaff and Williams to the small, mountain town of Prescott. We enjoyed a fine drive through some of the most beautiful scenery in the Southwest.

We found Mr. and Mrs. Williamson to be very interesting young people. We discussed the legends he had collected amongst the Indian people and we mentioned the flying saucers. We then looked over many clippings and numerous reports of this strange serial phenomena.

After our dinner, we decided to play a few parlour games. I had heard of automatic writing but had never actually tried it or even seen it done. Since my knowledge of it was small, I had never really formed any opinion regarding it. After all, we were just performing a parlour trick. Or were we? Two people were supposed to grasp a pencil held over a sheet of paper. The moment we started our stunt, the most amazing and incredible information began to appear on the paper!

My wife Betty and I had hardly ever mentioned saucers and certainly we never discussed automatic writing. At once, she was confused and somewhat upset. Before she had met the Williamsons she thought she had married a crazy man because of my weird interests. Now she was certain she had just met two more candidates for the State Sanatorium. But she was courteous and waited. We didn't have long to wait to see proof of the reality of our contact.

As I stated, I had always believed the saucers to be interplanetary in origin, but like everyone else I only knew what could be found in the daily papers and magazines. After discovering that Mr. and Mrs. Williamson had found ancient legends and accounts dealing with strange sky objects in the lore of primitive people, I really sat up and began to take notice. It was most interesting to know that these people of a bygone age had preserved knowledge of the very thing that today was causing such world-wide attention.

We realize that mature people do not take the results of parlour tricks very seriously. At first, neither did we; but the nature of the messages demanded that we investigate more thoroughly.

I feel that many ideas and impressions come to certain receptive minds that could only have their origin in that vast storehouse of all knowledge: The Universe. Perhaps many of our great discoveries came about in this way. It is the explorer in man that drives him ever onward to new knowledge of this Universe.

There are many things in this report that will not be readily acceptable to many. This is to be expected of any publication dealing with the flying saucers. The term saucer itself is a laughter-provoking word. How ironic this is! The greatest happening in the history of mankind and it was ushered into the world as a joke by many.

These saucers that fly in our skies come to us from that great beyond that we have not yet begun to explore. What could they teach us? We anxiously awaited their answers!

STATE OF ARIZONA }
           } ss.   AFFIDAVIT
County of Navajo }

We the undersigned, being first duly sworn do solemnly swear; that the Documentary Report of Interstellar Communication by Radiotelegraphy entitled: "THE SAUCERS SPEAK", is accurate and true. We have been witnesses to and participants in these happenings as listed in the above report. We also state that we are trained observers by the very nature of our various occupations. We agree that a fact is not a fact until it is proven; and that much time, effort and research has gone into the above report to prove beyond any doubt its statements to be absolute fact. Our work was carried on in the acceptable and standard form of scientific research employed by radio operators, anthropologists, and others. We also state that many tests were performed under exacting conditions.

We are thoroughly convinced that the "Flying Saucer" phenomena is interplanetary in origin; that the mission of these ships to our Earth is a friendly one; that the "saucer" intelligences have developed ESP (Extra-Sensory Perception) to a high degree; and that these intelligences are of the human race inhabiting other heavenly bodies and are now attempting contact with any inhabitants of the planet Earth who are receptive to the Universal Truth.

We also swear that we are not members of any organization (religious, scientific, etc.) that would in any way profit or gain from our research. We are not propagating a dogma or creed and none of us involved would gain by perpetrating a hoax.

This report is being given to the people of the world because the facts contained therein were not given to us for our own elucidation, but are for all those seeking and desiring Universal Truth.

That the undersigned Lyman H. Streeter, on oath deposes; that he received the messages in International Morse Code.

                            Lyman H. Streeter Jr.
                            Lyman H. Streeter, Jr.
                            Winslow, Arizona
                            Licensed Radio Operator, W7OJQ

Susan Streeter
Susan Streeter   *George H. Williamson*
Winslow, Arizona   George H. Williamson, Sc.D.
Housewife   Prescott, Arizona
                            Anthropologist

Betty Bowen
Betty Bowen   *Betty J. Williamson*
Winslow, Arizona   Betty J. Williamson, B.S. & B.
Student   Prescott, Arizona
                            Chemist and Anthropologist

Ronald Tucker
Ronald Tucker   *Alfred C Bailey*
Winslow, Arizona   Alfred C. Bailey
Student   Winslow, Arizona
                            Conductor, Santa Fe Railroad

                            Betty M. Bailey
                            Betty M. Bailey
                            Winslow, Arizona
                            Housewife

Subscribed and sworn to before me this 7th day of March, 1953.

                            Genevieve W. Scott
                            Notary Public
                            Winslow, Arizona

My Commission Expires 10/26/56

5 PARLOUR DIARY

Remember that this is a Documentary Report, and truth is almost always stranger than fiction. All happenings listed herein are true and factual. Some of the methods used to make contact are certainly alien to our present ways of thinking. The Radio Diary which follows this section, will be readily acceptable to many, and will give them an opportunity to make the necessary links to reality as we understand reality.

This report contains a timely message. We have decided to tell it exactly as it happened and to fictionalize none of the story. If the reader refuses to accept recent developments in the field of Parapsychology and the work of Dr. Rhine at Duke University, that is his or her privilege. But the fact that there is such a thing as Extra-Sensory Perception cannot be denied. Many well-known scientists and universities are conducting experiments in telepathy. They realize that if we probe deeper into the man non-physical, we may eventually discover more about the fundamental nature of the human being and his place in the Universe—where he stands in relation to the entirety.

When F. A. Mesmer first brought mesmerism (now known as hypnotism) into notice in Vienna, about 1775, he was pronounced a charlatan. For many years hypnotism was considered a magician's trick or the work of the devil. There are many people today who still consider it as such, but medical associations have recommended its use to physicians and dentists. And it is being used daily throughout the world by reputable men of science.

Automatic writing itself, belongs to the order of mediumship known as mental, but at first sight it appears to be of the physical order. One has only to remember how difficult it is to cultivate the art of writing to realize that at all times the co-operation of the individual's own mind, although not necessarily of his consciousness, is necessary. Automatic writing has often been produced by medical men from the patient's subconsciousness; and it is reasonable to conclude that the medium's subconsciousness is operative when such writing is impelled by an outside communicator. Researchers in the psychic phenomena field have claimed that this writing can either be from the medium's subconsciousness or it can be from some disembodied entity. If this is so, then we can understand how telepathy in the form of automatic writing could be accomplished between two living beings in the same plane of existence, but located in widely separated areas. Distance, whether two miles or two million miles, would not be an important factor.

We know now that this telepathic contact can be made with human beings of outer space without the use of ,my device such as a pencil. However, this initial contact needed something whereby those receiving the messages would not think it was the product of their own minds. They could more readily accept what was written down in front of them in black and white.

In his book, *Men of Other Planets,* Kenneth Heuer (Lecturer at Hayden Planetarium) says, 'We do not know all that there is to know about the nature of the universe, and we are only beginning to learn a little about the science of the human mind or soul and its operations, powers and functions. The distance from the earth to Mars is nothing where the transmission of the force of attraction is concerned; it is almost insignificant in the case of light, a few minutes sufficing for a wave of light to traverse those millions of miles. Experiments made in the domain of magnetism equally prove that space is nothing for the will power of a mesmerist; and one day it may be possible, through some great strides in psychology, to establish communication between two beings on two different worlds.'

At different stages in the reception of the following messages, we altered our method of contact at the request of the space intelligences. As stated above, our first contact was through automatic writing using a sheet of paper and a lead pencil. The second method was employed to make it easier on us, and to speed up the transmission of words. We took a large sheet of ordinary wrapping paper and drew on it the letters of the alphabet and the numbers from 1 through 10. This still did not prove entirely satisfactory, so we made what we later called the 'board.' It consisted of the same letters and numbers, plus the words 'Yes' and 'No' and a plus sign on the right side and a minus sign on the left side. These signs indicated positive and negative.

This was much easier than holding a pencil for a long period of time. A glass tumbler was inverted and used as a 'locator.' It moved over the paper surface with considerable ease. Since the letters and figures were now arranged in a circular form, the transmission was speeded up greatly. Messages received in the above manner follow:

2 August 1952

'Masar to Saras.' (After much questioning we learned that Masar was the planet Mars and Saras was our planet Earth. It is interesting to note that Saras or Saros means 'repetition' in the ancient Chaldean language.) By your year of 1956 there must be a new Saras. Bell Flight 9 (Crystal Bells are the saucers) should land on Saras in 1956. Organize yourselves. There must be peace of mind. You are all for a purpose. You have a destiny. Don't fight Universal Truth!

'You are a dead civilization. We want your co-operation. Time is limited. I am Nah-9 of Solar X Group. I am the leader of a contact group. We were seen over Southern California last night and early today.' (Sunday, 3 August, newspapers carried stories of Air Force jet fighter bases being alerted for instant pursuit of saucer objects. They had been seen over the Mojave Desert at 11:45 p.m., Friday night, 1 August, and Saturday morning at 12:14 a.m., 2 August. Our contact had told us this information before we knew they had been observed.)

'Good and evil forces are working now. Organization is important for the salvation of your world. Contact us as soon as you can.

'There is a mass of planets in the organization. Why are your peoples unbelievers? You have begun the research. The time is up to you! Look up into the skies above you, don't lose contact with each other...

'We are friends of those interested, but we are not interested in those of the carnal mind. By that we mean the stupid preservation of self; disregarding the will of the Creative Spirit and His Sons.

'Your world has been observed for over 75,000 years. A survey was begun long ago of this planet Earth. How can we deny the eternal verities; Life, God, the Creator's place in the divine scheme? How can we sit by and watch the progress of evil men on this blob, the Earth? Come now, if you wish the answers that all mankind has been searching for since time began. You are wishing for these answers.

'Our group will be a duplicate of yours. We represent the people of outer space, you represent your world Saras. Cycles are computed by a group for this known as "Timekeepers."

'We have not wanted to interfere with men of Saras before. All men must make their progress wherever they are. But we cannot stand by and see another waste.

'We are all of the same Creation! Warning! "There will soon be a destructive blast to be felt on Saras. "This is of your own manufacture. Evil planetary men, who abound, will attempt contact with evil men of Saras for destruction! The good men of Saras must unite with the ben men of Universe. (ben means good). Great destruction can be caused by your H-bomb. It could all come too soon. Some destruction will come for sure! We have been alerted. We repeat, it is most important that you organize.

'Jupiter-9999, Ankar-22 speaking: Bell Flight from Jupiter joining Masar. Jupiter now leading group. Mercury, Morning Star (Venus), Andromeda-26470 and Wolf-359 are also in group. There are all he (males) in our group. Yon must have a group for contact. Band yourselves together.

Kadar Lacu speaking: 'I am head of Interplanetary Council-Circle on Master-craft. I am elected from the Universe.

'Why don't you all go eat *now?* We were wondering when you were going to wake up to the fact you are hungry. We have stomachs too, and we are empty. Meet you here at 8:30 tonight. Signing off.'

We had eaten early and were now ready for a light lunch. The above shows that the saucer intelligences have a sense of humour. This was evidenced several times during contact with them. At 8:30 p.m. we again received messages:

'It takes much mind power for our thoughts to reach you on Saras in this manner. Again we say that you must be very well organized amongst yourselves. For better contact we suggest a powerful receiving set or radio. You should have your own set as our set is radically different. But we can reach you in this manner. Our people have trod your byways. Have you not seen us? Bell Flight-9 is a Masar flight to Saras. Masar means Mars. The name Mars has been passed down to you in legend, but it is known to us as Masar. By 1956 Bell Flight-9 will come to Saras. [It may have come secretly—Editor] We have chosen you as you have chosen us and we know what your purpose is. It has been known since the very beginning. You all have a job to do for this Earth. Some chosen ones will be removed from Saras. Separate black from white (races are not meant here) and only a few will be saved. This is to preserve Earthian thought beginnings. Changes can take place, however. Yes, there will be a new Earth! There is much we must cope with. Your actions and plans will be guided by the powers of the Universe with the Creative Spirit's guidance. The evil forces of darkness will tell you that you can die for all of the research you are doing. They will say you can be destroyed, so the *ben* can never accomplish a plan.'

At 9:40 p.m. we received the following:

'Ankar-22 speaking of outer space contact: You have read about the recent explosions on Masar. These were not of our doing but were caused by your atomic experimentation. This caused extreme volcanic eruptions on Masar. Our bells are saucers. Crystal bells. Mankind must awaken or there will be an end to your civilization. More sincere ones will be added to your group as time goes on.'

In December 1951, Mr. Tsunco Saheki, Director of the Mars Section of the Oriental Astronomical Association and Lecturer at the Municipal Planetarium in Osaka, Japan, observed strange phenomena on Mars. There was a strange bright spot on the Tithonius Lacus and a large 'snowstorm' over the south polar regions. He said that the theory that it was caused by Martian volcanic eruption or fire seemed most likely. However, volcanic activity has never been reported on Mars before. But that means it has never been observed during the history of astronomical observation, which began approximately in the seventeenth century with the use of the telescope. Of course it was never observed before! Our experimentation has caused it to occur now for the first time due to earth's atomic explosions!

Also, a huge greyish cloud, sixty miles high and nine hundred miles in diameter, was observed on Mars in January 1950. The only theory offered was that it was caused by an extremely violent explosion, possibly a volcano and volcanic ash cloud. Again they said that such volcanic activity was unknown in Mars history. A worldwide observation was ordered, but no progress in understanding the phenomenon was made. It was originally observed by two Japanese scientists.

6 August 1952

'Zrs, my name. Transmitting. We will leave more definite information with you soon. Signing off at 9:30 p.m.'

9 August 1952

'I am Regga of Masar, Council Circle meets. You were assembled tonight. Oara is here. He is the planetary representative of Saturn. I must tell you a few things of interest. These true facts may even surprise you, but they are so. Many of your people on Earth know them to be true. Your Sun, which is our Sun also, is not a hot flaming body. It is a cool body. One of our great astronomers believed this and stated it. The so-called solar prominences are as cool as your aurora borealis (northern lights). You do not necessarily have to have heat just because you have light. Look at your firefly. You think your Sun gives off great heat because you can "feel" it. Certain forces come from the Sun and when they enter the earth's magnetic field this resonating field causes friction. And from friction you get heat. There are other facts about the Sun I cannot tell you now. In outer space the Sun does not appear as bright as it does to you on Earth.'

10 August 1952

'Nah-9 here and also Zrs. Zrs is from Uranus. All planets are inhabited. Many moons are inhabited also. Planets were created to sustain the life of the human race. Your scientists are planning on going into space in rocket ships. You may get to your Moon, but not beyond that. Both of your Moons (yes, you have two; one is the `dark moon' of Earth. You never see it because of certain conditions) are within your own magnetic field. If you try to leave field with rocket power or atomic power you will be torn to pieces. Your first Moon is not as far away as you think. Your scientists say that the mean distance between the centres of the Earth and Moon is 238,857 miles. Distortion is present, they are wrong. Your first Moon has an atmosphere and water. Some of your scientists have observed snowstorms on the Moon. They have even seen meteors plunge through the Moon's atmosphere. There must be an atmosphere if they see them burn up. There are even inhabitants on the Moon! We have many bases of interplanetary nature there, also.'

At 12.13 p.m. Nah-9 again tried for a contact with us, but he claimed there was interference of some kind.

17 August 1952, 8.25 p.m.

'I am Zo. I am head of a Masar contact group, but my home is Neptune. I am going to Pluto soon. Pluto is not the cold, dreary world your astronomers picture it to be. Mercury is not a hot, dry world, either. If you understood magnetism you would then see why all planets have almost the same temperatures regardless of distance from great Sun body. Sister rites are Universal rites. They are rotting. Earth is backward, too many wars. Peace to all men everywhere.'

'Regga speaking. Please put water on your stove to boil. It will help our contacting you at this time.'

'Zo again. "To apples we salt, we return." You may not understand this strange saying now, but someday you will. It is from one of our old prophecy legends. Rites will save your people. We are here to warn you. If there is dissension amongst you we will not contact you. Be calm and quiet! We have only love for all men. We hold certain councils on Uranus. We must now decide what to do about your planet Earth. Your bombs will destroy Universal balance. Your Hydrogen Bomb could make an asteroid belt out of you. This happened many years ago to planet of the fifth orbit. We knew what they were doing but we didn't interfere. We cannot stand by and see another waste. After their destruction there were terrible disasters on Masar. Great volcanic eruptions took place. Many of our people perished. We would have been thrown out of the Solar System and lost if we had not quickly constructed two artificial satellites. Some of your scientists have noticed that Phobos and Deimos reflect too much light to be made of earthy substance. They are right. They are metallic in nature. They readjusted our unstable condition and saved a planet.'

It is true that the ancient poets knew of the satellites of Mars before their discovery and ancient astrological works mention them. Jonathan Swift in *Gulliver's Travels,* 1726, wrote that Mars had two satellites and his complete description of them was most accurate. They were actually discovered as late as 1877 by Asaph Hall of the Naval Observatory in Washington. How did Swift and all these other individuals know that Mars had two moons? It seems strange indeed, and one can only make guesses.

'Touka of Pluto speaking: Sister towers interfere with our contact with you. Turn on your portable radio here in kitchen. You will hear us!'

This didn't make much sense to any of us. How could we hear them on a simple portable radio? And did they mean that the new radio station at Winslow, Arizona, was interfering?

'Regga : Friday and everyday we will try radio. We wait. Try to listen for us, and get a better radio, a more powerful set. Go to see Mr. R, a radioman. He will be all right if spoken to right. Tell him the truth, that you heard that if the saucers are from space they might be contacted by the radio. It is most important that you contact us by this means. That is what we meant before when we told you to contact us as soon as possible! Contact between 340 kc. and 400 kc. Get a telescope, if you can. It will be a sin to witness the bombs. Listen to the radio signals we are now giving to you. Bell Flight-8 is to Arizona. We eat. But go look for a radio set. We are happy. Try 400 kc. We may even talk to you! Go in your car to the railroad station. Ask there about someone who might have a radio set. Listen to us. We will be over Winslow 8-22-52, 7 miles altitude.'

A staff member at Lowell Observatory, Flagstaff, Arizona reported to a friend of ours that on 8-22-52 they would focus the large telescope for terrestrial observation over Winslow, but did not say what they were looking for or why. No mention was made of the source of information that caused this observation to be made. We thought this strange, indeed. Why would they be interested in something in our skies the very night Regga had told us they would be over Winslow?

We followed our instructions and went to the railroad station. We asked the telegraph operator on duty if he knew of a 'ham' operator who might co-operate with us. He gave us the name of a well-known licensed operator. We talked to him over the phone and asked him to listen on his receiver to 400 kc. and see what he could hear. We waited while he went to his set. Finally he came back to the phone and said, 'Some crazy guy is sending a series of V's, that's all.' We thanked him for his help and co-operation, and hung up. We then returned to the apartment, and when we turned on the portable kitchen radio, turned down as far as we could go, we did hear "····-" repeated several times. One of us knew 'C Q' in code so we asked them to send that over the radio if it was truly them. And sure enough, 'C Q' was immediately forthcoming! This was truly amazing. We could hardly believe what was taking place. But with their superior equipment this was understandable. We decided to continue with our crude 'board.'

'Zo speaking: I am on Bell Flight-8 at 50 miles altitude. We promise to transmit on 340 kc. to 405 kc. with International Morse Code 8-22-52 at 7 miles altitude.'

We wondered if Lowell Observatory's information source was as strange as ours. And were they instructed to look at the skies on 8-22-52 as we were instructed to listen on this date?

Now we were really excited ! Was it actually true? Would we really hear men of other worlds over Mr. R's receiver? Would they answer our many questions, and what message did they have for Saras? It seemed they did not want to give too much information over the 'board.' We now know that by establishing contact with us on radio they knew we would accept what they said. They knew that the 'board' messages did not prove their existence positively. No matter how startling the information was, they knew the materialistic phenomenon of code would go far in establishing their absolute identity. Someone had said we were in communication with low grade spirits. And that these spirits were having a good time by telling us weird lies. But we knew that spirits would not tell us to go to a radio set, for they would be cutting off their only means of communication with us. We felt sure these spirits couldn't use a radio transmitter and send us messages in International Morse Code!

Other saucer research groups had suggested systems of coloured lights to attract space craft. But we agreed with our newly found friends from space, that radio was by far the best method of contact. And what would it lead to? A personal face-to-face contact with men of other planets? We dared not have such high hopes, but we wondered!

Here at last would be positive proof that the flying saucers were interplanetary craft. It seemed hardly possible that by the use of a simple parlour trick, we had contacted other intelligent Universal individuals. On 22 August 1952 the strangest and most wonderful adventure of our life began!

6 RADIO DIARY

In our endeavor to establish radio contact with the flying saucers or other space craft, a radioman whom we called Mr. R was contacted by Al. This man had a great deal of experience in his field and held a commercial license as well as an amateur ham license. Mr. R was skeptical, but quite willing to try a contact. Arrangements were at once made to listen on Friday evening, 22 August 1952

All messages received by radiotelegraphy will be capitalized throughout this Diary. All other messages (from the 'board,' etc.) will be in small letters enclosed within quotation marks.

On the evening of 22 August 1952, Mr. R saw what he thought was a very small meteor display over Winslow, Arizona. He also observed what appeared to be a very bright light traveling at a high altitude in the sky above him. He turned on his receiver to 400 kc, and many strange signals were heard but not identified. Al, Mr. and Mrs. R were in the R's kitchen later when they all suddenly heard strange, clear code signals coming to them. They all thought it must be coming from the radio shack in the backyard, but when they went to check, there was nothing to be heard there. After they came back to the kitchen, the mysterious code was heard again! It seemed to be coming from the very air itself!

About 2:00 a.m., 23 August 1952 code signals were again received. Mr. R said it sounded as though two people were talking back and forth to each other using code. However, he said it was a code unfamiliar to him. He couldn't make any sense out of it at all. This strange code used a system of dots and dashes. After all, what else could be devised? It seemed there were more of these dots and dashes used for each letter or symbol than are used in our standard International Morse Code. Mr. R had his pencil and pad before him, and he hoped he might be able to make some sense out of the code coming over his receiver in loud, clear tones. Then he suddenly wrote down ZO, and in a few minutes, AFFA He turned and asked Al if those words meant anything to him. At this time, the name Zo was very, understandable, but the name Affa was not. Nothing else was heard of an identifiable nature.

23 August 1952, 5.18 p.m.

'Regga speaking. You made contact with us on radio yesterday. I think Lowell Observatory saw us.'

'This is Zo. It wasn't altogether our fault that we didn't make a good contact last night. Affa was talking to me last night. He helps us in many ways. Soon there will be another contact. You have already had good contact with us. Be patient! Affa is from the planet Uranus. He was listening in last night. Be careful... 40 meter band is all right. We will do our best on radio contact.

'Affa of Uranus tries to keep us from talking to you. Uranus doesn't believe in too much contact with the Earth planet. Affa told me not to let you hear us, but I arranged it so you could hear something. He interfered then, but helps otherwise. He was afraid of Lowell Observatory. The 'big eyes' were looking at us, and they are doing special work up there on the mountain now. They have installed certain types of electronic equipment.

'California earthquake was caused by your planet's magnetic disturbances. We must tell you about Orion. Many there wish to conquer Universe. We are here to warn you of this also. However, we find few receptive persons on Saras. You are helping us now by what you are doing.

'Nah-9 speaking: The Orion Solar Systems are much like Saras. The principles of good and evil are universal. Saras is the lowest in progression in your Solar System, but there are planets in the Creation that are above you and below you in state of progression. There is no beginning or end; no big nor small; no low nor high estate. We are all on the road to All Perfection. We must tell you that Orion is coming soon to Saras in a square star body. The year of decision is soon to come to you! We will be seen by more and more people in 1953, We want to land and you can be of help to us. Will you? We are happy. Be patient, for you were lucky you even heard us on the radio the other night. Affa is afraid Saras is too evil. You wonder how long our space flights take us. It takes only a few minutes to go from Masar to Saras. We do not fly as you think of flying, but we drift or glide on magnetic lines of force. We need no fuel. We operate in a Resonating Electromagnetic Field just like planetary bodies do. Now we are hungry as you are. Sometimes on Neptune we eat Macas. They are similar to your cattle, but they do not have horns and they have very big ears.'

'This is Zo. It is now 8:00 p.m. your time. Garr of Pluto is on Saturn. Bell Flight-9 could be sooner than 1956 to Saras. It all depends on future conditions.'

'Regga: Be tactful in regards to everything you do. Remember you are dealing with Saras. We join you, it's us. Mr. R must try, try, try. Important now, perhaps only chance. We will tell you more by radio. A landing can be arranged. Our superiors must decide. Fate of all creation here depends on it.'

We all wondered what our brothers from other planets looked like and they gave us some information. However, they, are usually reluctant to speak of themselves, for they feel that they are here to serve and there are many other important services to be rendered at this time.

'"This is Zo again. I am 5 feet 7 inches tall, and I weigh 148 pounds. I have auburn hair. I am what you would call 25 years old. I am married. I have seven children. We have marriage mates from birth. But you shall see us for yourself someday! We want to give you a code so that we can locate you on radio. Please have Mr. R transmit E U. We will then transmit DA. EU equals Saras and DA equals Outer Space Contact. Mr. R knows more than he tells. He has tried to contact us for about two years now. He never succeeded, however. He tried too high and the time was not right yet. We do have a good life where we are, but wait to ask about that. One of you is interested in our musical instruments. Yes, we do have them. We call them tonas. Mr. R is fine. He is interested in us. We will be on your first Moon tonight. By the way, the craters on your Moon were not caused by meteors nor were they caused by volcanic action. They came about by vortical motion. Use radio. We must contact you. Try 40 meter band to transmit. Receive on 405 kc. The bands may vary at times, but keep trying. Keep listening.'

'This is a member of Masar Flight speaking. Saturn Tribunal has given permission for a possible landing. Uranus has to be won over in Universal Tribunal. Saturn is the seat of justice, but not "justice" as you know it. Orion systems want to destroy. You have more than nine planets in your Solar System. Patras is next beyond Pluto, and there are twelve all told.'

'Zo again. I will be staying at base on first Moon tonight. We usually take no women on our survey or scientific trips. There are several types of space craft. One is a Scout Craft holding one or two men that appears to fly upside down and has an antenna-like projection on the bottom; another is an arrow-shaped or crescent-shaped craft, it is a Master-Craft for it will guide many crystal bells in mass flight formation; then there is the Mother-Ship that you call a cigar-shaped craft. These latter can be many miles in length and send out the green 'fireballs' to explode, then photographs of the magnetic fault lines can be taken. You would be astonished if you knew what these fireballs really were. They are not the same as your remote-controlled devices. Most bells do not travel between planets, for they are carried within the Mother-Ships. There are ships that look like tubes; craft that are round with an opening in the centre; and triangular-shaped craft. Some of these ships have a high intensity field and others have a low intensity field. The flatter the form, the more intense the field of the craft. The small discs a few inches in diameter are in the fireball class although they are not all used for the same purposes. Saras is like a space ship. We operate the same way. Look and listen. We know what life is. There is no death, for all life is eternal. Peoples of Saras are afraid of death. But it should be a time of rejoicing for a soul has gone on to greater progressions. Pray for the salvation of Creation. Good night, my beloved friends.'

This message from Zo gave all of us a warm, friendly feeling. A stronger bond existed after this night between those above and us. We were amazed at the high intelligence of Zo. He was, indeed, a very fine young man. We knew that we no longer needed to fear these space intelligences. Although we hadn't actually feared them, we nevertheless had been aware of the unknown. What would we discover? Would it be beautiful or would it be horrible? Now we knew. On the other planets of our Solar System there was beauty. On Saras there was horror.

24 August 1952 (11:40 a.m.)

'This is Actar of Mercury speaking. We are the radio centre for this Solar System because of our nearness to great Sun. We are now on your first Moon. Zo is here, also. Did you know that your blue sky of Earth is due to the Resonating Electro-Magnetic Field? It is the reason your stars twinkle near the horizon and give off so many colors. Your scientists do not know what causes this. Some on Saras know what Chinvat is. Your scientists claim that the Solar System had its beginning in a big cloud of gas and dust. They call this the Nebular Hypothesis. Others speak of the Planetesimal Theory where the sun was supposed to have come closer to another star. But they do not agree on any of these ideas. They must honestly admit that they do not know how the earth and the other planets came into being. Did you know that comets are really planets, however. Planets are made like a snowball rolling down a mountain, and they get bigger and bigger.'

'Zo speaking: We can't be sure of contacts ahead of time. Listen at 405 kc.; 40 meters; EU answer back. We want to be sure of everything before we land. Look for others to help our landing. Cosmic conditions (right?) now. Uranus will agree to plans if all parties are in complete co-operation. We just had a meeting and decided. Radio contact is good, but this method (the 'board') is not very satisfactory. On your regular radio there is too much of sordid life, just like Saras. (One of our wives said that she liked the soap operas on radio and the answer was, "Pooh!") Earthians don't think. That's why they are in such a mess now. Check? Patras No. 10-QM interfering. We will clear airwaves, wait. Back on the Moon at 12:30 p.m.'

Many times, the facts told us by our contacts, were later confirmed. Upon questioning, Mr. R did admit that he had become very interested in the possibility of Interstellar Communication after he read an article on this subject in QST, one of the amateur ham radio magazines. He said he had attempted some sort of contact on a high frequency and a short wave length.

A friend of Mr. R, a man high up in radio circles, told him that he had also received strange signals at various times and definitely believed it to be from space intelligences. One day this friend called Mr. R and told him that Lowell Observatory did see the saucers on Friday, 22 August 1952. This confirmed what Zo had told us before.

On 2 August 1952 they had told us they had been seen over Southern California. The newspapers of the next day told us exactly the same thing! We learned later that a young man in Los Angeles, California, had made a personal contact with the saucers on the same day, 2 August 1952. The space friends were really working hard at this time. It seemed sightings were being made everywhere, perhaps they were going all out on their 'Project Saras,' trying to find receptive minds.

25 August 1952 (9:25 p.m.)

Another attempt was made to establish a more lasting contact with our space friends. We were in the radio shack at Mr. R's. He transmitted EU so they could locate him. Almost immediately a very loud signal came in on the receiver.

'THIS AFFA. SWAP TO 450 KC.'

Mr. R quickly changed from 405 kc. to the requested 450 kc. At first we did not know what he was receiving after the switch, for he suddenly jumped up from his seat, almost ran through the closed door, and dashed outside. He was very excited and called to us to come out quickly. He had climbed tip on top of his ham shack and was scanning the sky.

We asked him what the message was. After he told us we understood the exuberance of his action. He had received: 'COMING IN. COMING IN. COMING IN.' Mr. R thought they meant they were coming in close to Earth and he wanted to get a view of them if possible. We looked and looked but saw nothing. Then, as we all stood on top of the shack, we heard another message coming in over the receiver. We were very quiet so Mr. R could hear the code. This time it was: 'LOOK FOR A DARK SPOT IN THE, SKY. LOOK FOR A DARK SPOT IN THE SKY. LOOK FOR A DARK SPOT IN THE SKY.' Then we all saw a strange, dark object towards the south in the Milky Way. This object stayed in that position for some time, but it was gone at the end of an hour.

While we were still outside another message came in, but it was not as loud as the others and it faded out to such an extent that Mr. R did not receive all of it. 'TO US ANOTHER TIME WHEN—.' The last message was signed off with: 'DA DA K DA.'

We decided at once to try the board. Perhaps we could obtain more information from its use.

'This is Zo. Look for us in the west. You will see a steady blue light. The dark spot in the sky was Affa. Keep trying radio. The name of my mate (wife) is Um. She is from Masar. There is a Solar System with the name Twenty-two. This is because there are 22 planets. Elala is the name of Planet 15.'

We looked for the blue light in the west and did see it. It was gone in about twenty minutes.

'Regga of Masar. We wish to clear up certain things. These are things you have been wondering about. You wonder if we have advanced in medical science. We have not. We have no disease! Disease-ridden bodies are caused by man's wrong living. We are ahead of you in development. You Earth people are always thinking in terms of years. But in your years we are many thousands of years ahead of you. Venus is farther ahead yet, and other planets even more so. We of Masar are next to you in progression. We have slight change in seasons, the other worlds have perfect weather at all times. We have great powers, but we have not destroyed each other because we have followed the Infinite Father. You have not. Yes, you have many churches and seem to worship what you call God. But you worship by word, not by deed. You say, "Peace is for the strong." Your Holy Book tells you, "The meek shall inherit the earth." "Thou shalt not kill," yet you kill. One came and said to you, "Turn the other cheek." But you do not. Your government contacted us a few years ago. They would like to know our secrets, but they never will no matter how hard they try.'

The radio contact we were now receiving was the great turning point in our research. Now we knew for sure that we were in contact with men from outer space! We were practically unknown so far as the world was concerned, but they were willing to contact us because we desired to know more about them. We wanted to listen and find out if they knew the answer to what the entire world was asking: Can world peace be a reality? The ones that should have been listening were interested only in discovering the secret of saucer propulsion. In all publications one could only find poor reasoning and logic as one so-called 'authority' would ridicule another. The Government itself was contradictory in its statements. There seemed to be much confusion in high places. As of 25 August 1952, Captain Ruppelt of Project Saucer (now known as Project Bluebook and Project Twinkle), said more competent observers than ever before have been reporting saucers. The Captain, who started as a one-man agency, now has eight fulltime assistants. The Air Force is buying a hundred special cameras, which it hopes will help determine what the provocative objects are made of, and it is considering buying several photographic telescopes of a new type, costing as much as five thousand dollars apiece, with which a continuous photographic record can be made nightly of the sky over the whole hemisphere. After several years and nearly two thousand reported sightings of a serious nature, there is no discussion in Air Force circles of abandoning the pursuit of the elusive saucers. If the saucers are a joke, then the Air Force had better stop paying for such expensive equipment with the taxpayers' money.

26 August 1952

Many of our radio messages are incomplete. This can be readily understood when one considers the great speed of transmission used by the space craft. Mr. R, although a fine radio operator, could hardly keep up with the code given. He said that there was no variation in dots and dashes. In other words, it sounded as though the code was being sent over a mechanical transmitter. Also, many of the words were incorrectly spelled. On closer examination it was found that they were spelled more or less phonetically. When the coded messages would come into Mr. R's receiver, they blocked his set. If there happened to be a weaker code coming in from elsewhere at the same time, it was automatically ridden over. If Mr. R had turned up full volume, it would have been impossible to remain in the ham shack because of the intensity of the sound.

Several years ago when Mars came very close to Earth, radio silence was observed every hour on the hour for five minutes, and strange code signals were received by the FCC at that time. They have never been decoded and are now on record in the Bureau of Standards, Washington, DC. It is now known that a few years ago other messages were received just as Regga had told us they were. Yet, this information had been kept from the people. Why? We dare not answer this question! Much information is labeled under that frightening word: National Security. It seems there are those who fear that interplanetary recognition might mean extra-terrestrial allegiance. In other words, in the light of truth, the 'jig' is up!

The message received by Mr. R On this night follows. He was again listening on 405 kc.

'AM NSYKK YAM DE BEK VVK DE AFFA WWAS WWAS SAMT TK VVVVVV AWAS VVVVV VVVVV VVVV AWAS VV AFFAS K AFFAS WAIT AFFAS KMS ZO ZO WAS AFFA ZO OR ANS. DE DE DE DE DE DE DE DE DE DE DE W DE DE DE WMAS DE DE DE WMAS WMAS ANS ON 2.19 ANS 2.19.'

At this point there was a pause for several minutes while the weather report and aircraft came in. Then the message continued.

'TAKE UT GEE CT DAW AIUN KATTC A UAR JY YOU O E OZ CIAR NMOU IT R YOU WILL SEE US WH NO WIZ NML STCNA IZ ON BETTER TIME WHEN K SHOWS US WHEN YOU ARE READY TO VENTURE C KFPS HM. KI KS NBZS. KKSK KKSK KKZO KRON KRON KTUF KTUF KTZO KTZO KVDE KVDE KVQP LVE LVE TEK.'

Mr. R had been listening on 405 kc when the following message came through instructing him to change to 450 kc. As soon as he did, the message continued.

'450 TE SA AFFA SWAP YOUR R 450 K SWAP T I ARE YOU APPEAR TO YOU LATER WHEN AS OR SHIP COMPREHEND DA DA K SE WID26 EE WID26 Q QRA WID26.'

At this point Mr. R asked them the name of their station.

'I RST 57 QRA DE WID26 QRA RRR3 BL.'

(End of transmission).

'II SWWAS Y CT ZO DE ZO DE ZO K K OK II ZO AFFAS Y II II MT WNWA II ZO ZO YANT NW YN WI. WONT BE THERE UNTIL 1420 CMT KMC KTK RRB FLG INW IMH. FROM MASAR: YOU WILL SEE US IN THE SUN AT HIGH TIME TOMORROW VV THIS CAN BE THE SALVATION OF SARAS, IF ALL PLANS GO ACCORDING TO OUR WILL CAN YOU. II KA KARAS IS STILL IN THE AT. WE SHOULD BE IN YOUR AT. TOMORROW IF ALL GOES ACCORDING TO PLAN WITH COUNCIL.'

On 40 meter band Mr. R asked, 'Can you give us a sign tomorrow"

'YES YES ZO MAYBE IF YOU CAN GET A GLASS CAN BE BY SOLAS AT HIGH TIME SEEN BY LOW. THIS TIME CANT BE SURE DANGER TO OUR 450M COULD USE AGAIN. THIS WILL BE YOUR LAST CONTACT UNTIL SATURDAY WHEN YOU WILL HAVE TWO VISITORS FROM OUTSIDE.'

This was a message from Mars! We had thought radio communication with space craft possible, but direct contact with another planet never! Of course, our messages were probably relayed to Mars by the space craft using their superior equipment. Surely the people of outer space were interested in every man, woman and child on Earth.

Evidently they meant for us to obtain a telescope and look at the sun at noon. And did they mean that Lowell Observatory was watching? They had told us the Sun was a cool body so we could understand what they meant. Mr. R was amazed and very excited. What had they meant by, 'You will have two visitors from outside?' For a moment he thought it was possible two people from outer space were going to pay him a visit. He turned to Al questioningly and said, 'Are you expecting any company Saturday?' Al told him that Mr. and Mrs. Williamson were coming to Winslow from Prescott for the weekend. How did Mars receive this information? We wondered!

The above radio message is of great interest when considering what happened on Wednesday following.

27 August 1952

The evening newscasts carried the following story. At 12.00 noon a large fleet of aluminum-colored saucers were sighted over Yuma, Arizona. Also, over Yuma at the same time, a jet fighter pilot and his jet plane crashed to the ground. The cause of the accident was claimed to be unknown!

28 August 1952

The *Los Angeles Times* carried a very interesting article on this date. The astronomers at Mt. Wilson Observatory had observed strange, gigantic sun-spots on the sun around noon, 27 August 1952. The report stated that these spots were extremely large and that this was a very rare happening as it was now a period of declining sun-spot activity ! Instead of these spots lasting the usual period, they were gone the very next day!

Was this the sign they had promised us for High Time? We knew that many observatories were doing considerable research on this saucer problem. The 200-inch Hale telescope on Mt. Palomar, California, was supposed to be probing the vastness of the outer universe. Yet, in October 1952 they spent their time at Mt. Palomar looking over the Moon, Jupiter, Saturn, Mars, and other bodies of our own Solar System. Why all the sudden interest in the neighboring planets? Was it all to discover some outpost of the space intelligences? We wonder, yet we know that everything this great telescope has discovered has not been made public.

On the evening of 28 August 1952 the Bailey's took a drive from Winslow to Prescott to visit us (Mr. and Mrs. Williamson). They saw eight or nine objects in the southwest sky. They seemed to be traveling at a high rate of speed in a V formation.

At 11:30 p.m. in Prescott, Arizona, we again made contacts by the board.

'Regga speaking: The sun-spots were a sign to you. We help. The plane at Yuma was an accident, we did not shoot him down. The jet got too near our magnetic field. He saw us. Be patient with Affa, he hasn't learned English well. He is fine. We will do our best. Be careful. All is up to you. We travel speed of light at times. Your scientists say it is 186,000 miles per second. That is correct in some cases, but it is not constant, it varies. Our ships operate on east-west and north-south force lines.'

'This is Zo. Our worlds have the same atmosphere as yours. Some men of Saras will make visits someday to our worlds. There are certain men trying hard to contact us, but we will not pay any attention to them. Mr. R was sceptical at first. Remember, Orion is evil. The movie, *The Day the Earth Stood Still* was for a purpose and was more fact than fiction. Watch all nature for signs of catastrophe. The signs, such as tornadoes, earthquakes, floods, and so on will come to Saras soon and will get worse as time goes on. USSR is aware of us, too. Earth's last mile, we sad. It is impossible to reason with the peoples of Earth. Soon all could end here. Some will not see it, except from elsewhere, from outside.'

30 August 1952 (12:55 p.m.)

During our radio contacts there were usually eight or nine witnesses present in Mr. R's ham shack. Those listed on the affidavit are: Mr. R; Mrs. R; Betty Bowen, student; Ronald Tucker, student; George H. Williamson, anthropologist; Mrs. Betty J. Williamson; Mr. Alfred C. Bailey, Santa Fe Railroad conductor; Mrs. Betty M. Bailey. Others present at various times were relatives and friends. Al's mother, Mrs. Geraldine Bailey of Los Angeles, California, was present on several occasions. She has followed a very dogmatic religion all of her life, yet the very nature of the radio contacts opened her eyes to much truth of a Universal nature. She is now completely convinced of the authenticity of our contacts by radiotelegraphy.

Mr. R thought there existed the possibility that a hoax was being perpetrated on him. He was now certain of the sincerity of all of us, but perhaps some other ham had been sending the 'space' messages. He has a calculating, scientific type of mind and he wanted to be sure. If it was true he wanted to continue with it. If it was a hoax he wanted it to end, and quickly. We felt his skepticism was justifiable. After all, truth will stand any test.

One night, in the radio shack, Mr. R decided to try a test. He told none of the witnesses present what he was going to do, not even his own wife. In fact, he finally told us about a week after the happening. He needed plenty of time to think it over. This test was of such a nature that, if the messages were a hoax, they would have been revealed as such immediately. He was seated at his radio set, with his back to all those present. He had sent a question over his transmitter on the 40 meter band and he received an answer. Without any warning he quickly switched to 160 meters and asked another question. To his surprise, an answer was soon forthcoming! Any radioman knows that no power on Earth would have enabled any operator to know where he was switching to! Even if Mr. R had told the other operator that he was going to switch to 160 meters, still they would not have found him on that band until after the question had been asked. And, of course, they couldn't have answered the question if they hadn't heard it! An operator cannot make such a switch without telling what he is going to do and then giving plenty of time for the other side to find him on the new band.

The space intelligences really passed this simple, but very exacting test. This proved one of two things: Perhaps the space friends were using telepathy. Why not? If they are far ahead of us in development they have possibly acquired proficiency in Extra-Sensory Perception. It is also possible that their superior equipment allows them to receive no matter what band is used in communicating with them. It really matters little how it was accomplished. The important thing is that it was done! This was undeniable proof to Mr. R. He no longer had any doubts in his mind; he wanted to learn more.

'This is Zo speaking. We might even talk over radio to you soon. Use radio tonight on 450 kc. Or 405 kc. All on Moon. Council meets. Interested researchers represent Saras, as you do.'

'Affa is here. Oarhae retto! We speak the original language. We call it the Mother or Solar Tongue. The Solex Mal. Peoples of Saras spoke this Universal language long ago. Your Holy Book tells you the story of this. Your linguists will tell you that all languages appear to come from a common language. They do not know what this language is, however. It is closely related to the most ancient languages on Saras and antedated them. It is a symbolical pictographic language. All men of other worlds speak this language. You are a divided people, and you speak many tongues.'

'This is Kadar Lacu. I am head of the Universal Tribunal. I am now on the Planet Hatonn in Andromeda.'

'Regga speaking. We will try hard to see you soon. Greetings to Mr. R. Try 405 kc. and 450 kc. Our sets are quite different, but we contact you. Your government knows who we are.'

We had planned a radio contact for the night of 30 August 1952 since we were present as the radio contact had said we would be. We believe failure resulted because of the unexpected visitor who came to the ham shack. There was a great deal of confusion, while we tried to explain to him the nature of what we had been receiving. He was the type of person who refuses to believe in saucers or extra-terrestrial people. If one landed in front of him, he would explain it away. Anyway, the radio was silent this night.

31 August 1952

'This is Zo. Try not to be unattentive tonight, please. Concentrate. Send EU often over radio so we can locate you on beams of ionized particles. We can direct a beam straight to your antenna. We can locate you from ends of Omniverse.'

'Actar speaking. Certain great powers in your world wish to see us go away or see us destroyed. Neither will happen. These powers fear us, and when you fear anything you hate it. All planets have come to help certain ones on Saras. Those of the right mind are one with us! We will not harm anyone, only their own thoughts can do that. Evil destroys evil. Bounce back! Certain seeds have been placed on Saras. To the apples we salt, we return.'

'Kadar Lacu, my brothers. I am several hundred years old. A mere youth. The time has come to reveal these things to you. If man would only realize that he should love his brother.'

'Be at attention. I am Ponnar, a Universal Head. I am on Hatonn.'

'This is Sedat speaking. I am the Universal Record Keeper. Your records and those of many others are here on Hatonn in the Temple of Records. The planet known as Elala was once called Wogog.'

'Ponnar again, we are very strong now. Magritonic waves at pitch of 999887 and micomitronic vibrations can tear a radio receiver to pieces if not used correctly. Mr. R wonders why we have not contacted well-known scientists. We have contacted them, but many will not listen. They think Universal laws are insane. Garr of Pluto is here, also Oara of Saturn and Zo, he is on Moon. More detonations soon, more disasters on Saras. Quickly, not too much time left. Worlds can end. Many scientists will refuse to continue work on bombs.' (Later, 9,000 physicists signed a petition against the use of atomic energy.)

Although we tried desperately for radio contact this night, we received nothing. One very loud signal came in about 9:10 p.m. and completely blocked Mr. R's set. It lasted for about 15 seconds. It is possible it was a space craft, but nothing of value was learned from it.

A strange reddish light like a fireball flashed across the northern Arizona skies about 9:28 p.m. It was viewed in Albuquerque, New Mexico; Kingman, Arizona; and Prescott, Arizona. In Albuquerque, the fireball appeared bluish-green. The CAA reported it had received radio reports of the strange object from planes in the air at the time.

1 September 1952 (12:45 p.m.)

'Kadar Lacu. Too many people last night. Much confusion. Fewer the better for mind concentration. Otherwise conflicting thoughts. We have not traveled all the way to Saras to give misinformation. Many receptive people of Saras have been living with those who are doltish for too long. Seeds may be planted but they can rot and never reach maturity.'

'Ponnar speaking. Do not think of us as Gods. We are men like yourselves. We are only far ahead of you in progression. What we are today you can be tomorrow. The Creative Spirit is greater than man. At mention of His name, all worlds should bow. Do not speak of Him lightly. When it is safe we shall come in on radio. If you knew how soon destruction could come to Saras you would go screaming through the streets! We have saved your world several times already. The United Nations would believe certain men, if catastrophes were foretold before they happened. Maybe certain men will be raised for this duty. It is later than you think! You must at all times try to be in harmony with each other. Love one another, my friends.'

3 September 1952 (8.23 p.m.)

'Ponnar speaking. There are now many young people in your world who understand our message. They will accept it quickly for they are of the New Age. The Great Awakening is here. Many of our people are in your world now, and many people of Saras have been taken to outer space through the years. There is a young man in Ohio you must contact. He is of the right mind and heart. Many will not believe, but there are many who have received information as you have, and they will be joyous to know of your work. The so-called meteor seen Sunday over your area was us. It was a ball-globe being on its duty. We will be seen in the skies often. But do not strain to see us. When it is right for you to view us, you will. Our love to you all.'

11 September 1952 (5:30 p.m.)

'This is Zo. We will soon be at our meeting place on Fowser, the "dark" moon of your Earth. You are wondering about the Cosmic Dust cloud that you have heard shall soon come to Saras. Yes, this is true. It will come. And it will darken the Sun and Moon. Strange things will happen in your world. Great meteors shall be seen in the skies. I hope we might have a landing soon. Try radio again soon. USSR has been doing research in magnetic science. Recently many scientists were destroyed in Baltic area when a terrific explosion took place there. You will always notice a drop in temperature after these explosions. Oara of Saturn is here. You must know that Saras is a Masar name for your planet. Others call your world Chan. (Chan is very similar to certain ancient words meaning, 'afflicted'.) If we can arrange a landing do not fear impostors. You can be sure it will be us. On Hatonn your records can be seen. All thoughts are recorded there. Crystals are valuable to us. With a crystal miracles can be performed. Do not forget that there are evil forces. They will try to break you up, but stay together now, for the time is close. Do not get sidetracked. End soon, time short.'

At 9:00 p.m. we received a wonderful message from the Saturn Tribunal. It humbled us and made us realize that it was very necessary for us to be of one mind.

'Zo again. As time goes by, the way will be made harder and harder to make contact with us for evil will be pushed closer and closer to Saras. Therefore, we must make landing contact soon. Be very careful. You may go your own way if you wish, but you know what we have told you. If you believe us you will act accordingly. What you do with this knowledge is up to you. What we have told you will all come to pass. No man knows the hour, but it will come. Others have been told, but they went the way of all flesh on Saras. That is why we have been around for so long. Evil forces are always strong. Human nature has always fought this forbidden knowledge. Forces play on human frailties. Many have known in centuries past, but they either go insane because they could not live Universal Law or because they could not meet change. All changes but change itself. Few have been receptive, but you have been. Therefore, we have been interested in you. You know what must be done, so do it. We will do our part if you do yours. If there is disharmony amongst you, we are confused and cannot make definite plans. We must know what you intend to do. We told you over the radio to show us when you are ready to venture. The blind of Saras are more blind now. People cannot see the handwriting on the wall.'

'Ponnar. Look to Him for strength in this hour of universal doom. Without Him, all is lost. The Creative Spirit watches.'

'Kadar Lacu speaking. Do you realize what is at hand? Are our signs to you not enough? Every step you take is a part of a plan to further progress. Has not everything we told you come true?'

'Zo, my brothers. We happy to know all of you, but we are sad now. We hope you feel in heart as we do. We have told you that if it is possible for us to impress you, then evil forces can impress you too. Certainly you are not compelled to do as we say. But we must co-operate with each other. All must help. If there is one mind out of tune, all is lost. We did not intend for you to stay up nights. After all, you are adults now and must regulate your own daily schedule. There is work to be done, but when it is done is your own individual problem. We wait. We cannot fight opposition. After all, that is the trouble with Saras now. Men cannot get together and love each other. We are humble; want you to be humble, too.'

'I am Suttku, Judge of Saturn Council. We know what is in your minds.'

'This is Wan-4 of the Safanian Solar System speaking. We are pledged to those of receptive minds for all time past. But you can break the bonds tying us together if you will it. It is your choice, my friends.'

'Regga. You must decide now. Council waits. Worlds hang in balance. We can't wait much longer. Our time is short. If some of us must be sacrificed, then His will be done. We have come to Saras over millions of miles at a terrible cost. This has been because of our love for all men, everywhere. We are here to help those who wish to be helped. You have done nothing to displease us. But certain forces will try to discourage you in this undertaking that lies just ahead of you. Remember that weeks ago we told you to organize, be careful, and to be of one mind. The Universe awaits. Do you understand? We cannot do anything but good. Law of Universe. If we do anything but good, then we are evil. You want to do good, we know that.'

'This is Adu of Hatonn. You are given impressions on what to do. There are those on Saras who contact us this way. But you have not yet learned to separate your own thoughts from ours. Action speaks louder than words. That is an old Saras saying. We act, you act. Push-pull. Do whatever you think is right and necessary. We will guide you with the help of the Infinite Father.'

'Zo. We will not tell you what to do. Up to you. Council waits. What are you going to do? Plan. We must know. Then decide your steps. Be positive now. We can land soon. Certain conditions are necessary. You know what. Our regards to you. We cry, we are sad…. No one will listen to us!'

'Ponnar. We help you. All will be lost on Saras. All men's dreams and ambitions gone in a second. We are trying to help, that is why we are here. Uranus is still unsure. We go. Look for us later tonight. Go now to first Moon. Salutes! Good-night, my friends.'

15 September 1952 (9:30 p.m.)

On 13 and 14 September 1952, loud, strong signals were picked up by Mr. R. However, no code came in.

'Ponnar speaking. The Cosmic Dust Storm is true, I confirm its coming to Saras.'

19 September 1952 (6:30 p.m.)

'Zo again. Ro from the Toresoton Solar System is here with me and wishes to greet you. We walk the streets, but cannot come to visit with you in your home just yet. We cannot say why. We have friends on Elala, Planet 15 in Solar System 22. The Four Great Primary Forces are: Static Magnetic Field; Electro-Static Field; Electro-Magnetic Wave; Resonating Electro-Magnetic Field. Your scientists do not understand the last one mentioned. We have a symbol for this in the Solex Mal. It is similar to your so-called swastika. The Four Forces coming out of the Creator. It is one of the most ancient of Saras symbols. That is not strange. It is because the ancient people of your world understood nature and this knowledge has since been lost to you.'

20 September 1952 (8:30 p.m.)

'This is Zo. We can hear you no matter what meter band you send on. We have heard all the messages you have sent to us by radio transmitter, and more. We have impressed you from time to time, and will continue to do so. Now what I am about to tell you will seem foolish. It is the way we do things at times. This is so it will all appear in a most conventional manner. You were impressed to go and see a certain motion picture. You did not know that the cartoon was Bugs Bunny in *The Hasty Hare.* We mentioned Bugs Bunny to you several times before, but you thought it was foolish and did not enter it into your records. We had our reasons. This cartoon was about a flying saucer and its coming to Earth. You saw the letter held in the hand of the saucer pilot and you noticed that its date was 9-27. This date is important in 1952. You will see!'

'Actar of Mercury speaking. Mr. R is to transmit EU EU WE ARE READY TO VENTURE. Then we will answer. We will tell you whatever is necessary over your receiver.'

Since our space friends talked of a landing so often, we decided to have a picnic in the mountains and perhaps they would land for us. This way we could relax, away from the activity of town, and enjoy a fine week-end. If 27 September was important we wanted to be in on it. (Mr. and Mrs. Williamson arrived in Winslow on 26 September).

27 September 1952 (12:10 p.m.)

'Zo speaking. Try tomorrow for a landing as planned. Worlds can be saved. There is a meeting on Pluto. Kadar Lacu is there. Mr. R must try radio often. This contact must be a success.'

'Wan-4. Some of us are from distant systems. Oara, Actar, Ro, and Nah-9 send their greetings to you.'

'Suttku. We are assembling on Moon now. Danger to you as landing becomes a reality. Landing area you picked is not perfect, but good. We will circle area for several minutes first. We usually do this. We are feeling good over this, my friends.'

'Kadar Lacu again. Actar is with Nah-9 of Solar X Group in the ship, "Trocton." I am on Pluto. Masar will be in your atmosphere tonight. Try for radio contact for sure. Love.'

'Zo. Plan well to avoid slip-ups. Follow our instructions or we cannot come in. Some will try to trick us. Must be careful. Mr. R must try to be calm while at radio. He wants contact very much. Too much concentration is a block. We will protect the group. My wife, Um, is the first woman in her position to come into your atmosphere. She comes to help the women of group. Prepare yourselves quickly now. There must be harmony. Try hard. Do the best you can.'

'This is Lomec of Venus. I am with Terra on Ship-49 coming in to Saras. You will be contacted tonight by radio. Greetings to all.'

We had a short rest and continued our contact at 5:30 p.m.

'Zo. Many are here and greet you. Kadar Lacu had a meeting on Pluto with Touka. We are now several miles above you. 2:00 p.m. is all right for landing tomorrow. Be sure to try radio tonight. There must be no confusion. Watch. Worlds wait. My young son, Elex, greets you all. He is with me now. If you only knew what you did to your body by smoking you would quit at once! We never use tobacco. It is poison. Bell Flight of 200 craft from Safanian Solar System; 500 from the Toresoton Solar System. There are 14,000 bells near the second Moon, Fowser. We have many bells in our mother-craft.'

It was 5.30 p.m. when they told us they were over Winslow. At 5:55 p.m. we heard a tremendous swishing sound and a roar. The neighbors heard it also and couldn't figure out what it was. It was definitely not a jet plane. It was a sound that we couldn't recognize. It was more like the sound of a big beehive. After we went outside we saw them in the distance moving at great speed through the sky.

'Actar speaking. Try 405 kc. tonight. Ronem.'

'This is Um, wife of Zo. I have my own ship called, "Belga." Women do not ride with men on journeys to Saras because of the nature of such trips. My love to each and every one of you.'

'I am Noro, my brothers. Head of landing contact group. Here are instructions for you. Ship of Planet Masar will attempt landing Saras tomorrow at 2:00 p.m. Ship of Regga with Zo. Its name is "Clacteem." Many Crystal Bells over your world tonight.'

'Kadar Lacu speaking. I designed the ship "Clacteem." It is a special landing craft. We will have much to tell you when we see you. Our form will touch your form. It is the Father's plan. Mr. R may not wish to go. He is needed on Saras for a purpose. All of this is up to you. Whatever you wish to do.'

'This is Zago of Contact Group. When we land we shall say to you in the Solex Mal: "Tu Vec Satum Do Pattla Barraga." Then you will answer us by saying, "Udum Regan Vec Yonto Nictum Barraga." Vec means space. Barraga means friends.'

'Kadar Lacu again. Landing ship is being readied on Fowser. Big observatories of world look at Moon and see many craft there. They know they are not seeing locusts. Radio tonight.'

'Ponnar speaking. Soon I shall have beautiful words to say to you.'

In the evening we were at Mr. R's in the ham shack. We all felt that we would have a contact with our space friends, for they always told us the truth. Eight people were present besides Mr. R's father-in-law from Tennessee. He had arrived almost unexpectedly. The results of the radio contacts were astounding. We never dreamed that we would have such experiences. When the set was turned on we had almost immediate contact.

'AGFA AFFA SARAS IS LISTING 92° TO—. HERE IS THE PLANET OF SAGAFARIS CALLING SARAS. THIS IS THE PLANET OF SAGAFARIS CALLING SARAS. AGFA. VERY POOR CONDITION EXISTS. VVS VENIS VENIS. TFAS KS AR RAGIF KONT VA.'

When Mr. R received the message that the planet Earth was listing 92° he turned to us and said, 'I can't go for that.' However, it is obvious that they were not referring to our method of dividing a circle. The word Sagafaris was repeated several times each time it came in. By 'Very poor condition exists,' they were referring to Earth.

'SARAS PLESE SARAS PLESE V V VARY 92 HASTE.'

Mr. R quickly turned to 92 meters on the receiver. This band is used for aircraft communication. It seemed a speech was being given in a large auditorium. The static was terrible and we could only hear a word now and then. The voice was loud and masterful and spoke perfect English. There was reference to Germany and America and that they could no longer appeal to reason, etc. That is about all we could understand of the message. This was our first and last contact by radiotelephony. Because we did not have good reception on 92 meters, Mr. R switched back to 405 kc.

'OUR SECOND APPEASEMENT TO THE PEOPLE OF EARTH. SHORT WAVE BROADCAST. WE AWAIT, WE AWAIT. WHY BE IN SUCH — WHEN HASTE IS —. THIS MUST BE THE TIME. THIS MUST BE. HASTE, HASTE. WE CANNOT STAND BY AND SEE ANOTHER WASTE OF CREATION. THIS IS THE TIME. CANNOT FAIL. CANNOT FAIL. THIS CAN BE THE END OF ALL ON SARAS. THE LANDING WILL BE FOR SURE. SOON, SOON, HASTE. IS ALL IN READINESS' YOU MUST BE THERE SO MUCH DEPENDS 4 K-4. 40 MILES OFF K-4.'

There was a long pause before transmission began again. We couldn't understand what they meant by K-4. We thought it might refer to a certain area on a map. Would this mean they had changed their mind in regard to the chosen landing site? Mr. R finally asked them what K-4 was.

'SORRY NOW YOU MUST KNOW. K-4 SPACE SHIP OUTSIDE. THIS MUST BE A DANGER SIGN TO THE WONDER OF EARTH PEOPLES. THE LANDING WILL BE FOR SURE. WE DON'T CARE IF WE ARE SEEN BUT MUST BE ON THE WATCH, BE CAREFUL. WILL BE THERE IF NO OUTSIDE —. FROM MASAR.'

This does not seem to be a very long contact, but there may be many pauses before a complete message is received. The code itself is a wonderful thing to hear. The quality is very unusual and the speed of transmission is very fast. It was necessary for

Mr. R to request that they transmit slower if possible. They then sent about three words at a time, but the speed itself was in no way reduced. Perhaps, because of the nature of their sending device, they cannot slow down the transmission noticeably. Always, just before a message would come in, a loud signal would be sent. This was used to alert Mr. R so that he could get back to his set before the code began.

All of us had been trying to decide about Mr. R's father-in-law. The old gentleman thought we were going on a picnic the following day. Several of the women were helping Mrs. R in her kitchen prepare chicken, sandwiches, etc. Mrs. R didn't know what to do with her father. If she took him to the landing site, he might prevent the landing by his presence. Also, because of his extremely poor health he might suffer a heart attack if he saw a ship. On the other hand, if she left him at home, he would be alone and would think he wasn't wanted because he was old. She asked all of us what we thought she should do. We could reach no final decision in the matter. Suddenly, without Mr. R having to transmit a word, the code came in again.

'YOU SHOULD NOT.'

We believed that this was an answer to what we had just been discussing. We thought if we did take him to the landing site we would tell him all about our radio contacts and what to expect beforehand. Evidently they didn't want us to say anything to him yet. But how did they know what we had been thinking or saying. Mr. R had transmitted nothing! Did these space intelligences receive our thoughts? If we had stopped to think we would have known they did, for they contacted us by means of the board in the same manner. It wasn't any more unusual to do so by radio. We wanted to clear it all up, so Mr. R transmitted: 'What about elder B?' Then there was a long delay of about one hour and forty-five minutes. But the message they gave us was well worth waiting for.

'WITH CARE HIS MIND — SCARS — STILL RESTING. TRYING AGAIN. SAW SAGAFARIS. JUPITER TRYING TO GET MIND CORRELATION OF FATHER. MIND SCARS PREVENT THEM FROM SEARCHING DEEP. CANNOT REACH FULL PROBE. MAN IS ELDERLY. TOO MUCH PROBING MAY FUSE MIND. JUPITER CANNOT REACH YOU. RELAY FROM MASAR. STILL TRYING TO REACH FULL PROBE. MIND SCARS PREVENT. THERE WILL BE FOUND SALINE SOLUTION BY BED. PLEASE CLEAN. WILL HELP CHEMICAL COMPON — IN — NOW THIS - DEPTH OF MIND CAN BE REACHED IN — NEVER FEAR THE AGED THEY CAN HELP AGAIN WHEN THEY ARE BROUGHT TO LIFE. BODY CELL DETERIORATION NOT IN NECC — A POOR CONDUCTOR. QUALITY IN — WILL LET THIS GO BY TRIBUNAL ON SATURN. THEY WAIT FOR COMPLETE PROBE OF MIND. OUR K-4 :MOVING AWAY FROM THE — TO AWA AGFA AFFA REFIS LAQU. BETWEEN. ALL SOURCES MUST KEEP CLEAR OF ALL SPACE, THE SHIPS NUMBER 400 IN YOUR SKY. KADAR. 5555 5555 KALAR.'

The space intelligences couldn't have known that Elder B was Mr. R's father-in-law, yet they said they were trying to get a mind correlation of the father! Again, they had picked up our conversation and thoughts. Also, it seemed they had seen the space craft from Sagafaris. The old gentleman was asleep all this time inside the house. They knew this fact also. He suffers from excessive, frequent passage of urine and when Mrs. R went into his bedroom to check on him, she found the solution they said would be there! It was beyond belief ! How could beings as far away as Mars and Jupiter know what was going on inside a bedroom millions of miles away? Of course, there was a space craft nearby, but still many miles away. What powers these people must have! And what did they mean by, 'Never fear the aged they can help again when they are brought to life'' Did this mean that these space friends had the knowledge of life and death? Could they give us proof positive of life after death? These people had the answers to man's oldest questions!

Mr. R missed much of these messages because of speed of transmission and the very nature of them. He was astounded, as we all were. He said, 'If I ever doubted it, I don't now.' After a long pause again, another message came in.

'MASAR TO FRIENDS OF SARAS. BE OF PEACE. MIND PROBE IS NOT INJURING HIS REACTION TO SHIP. HE WILL RECOVER IF ANY SERIOUS RESULTS DO OCCUR. HE WILL NOT IF HE — IS ALL IN THE TRIBUNAL. THEY HAVE JUST MADE CONTACT WITH DEEP PROBE. CAN SEE NO HARM TO MIND. HE SHOULD BY ALL SENSE — B — WALK HIM TO SPOT AND IF APPEAR, TELL HIM WHAT IS EXPECTED. HE BELIEVES. IS WHAT YOU CALL IQ CAN BE GREAT DEPTH IN — HAVE IN MIND GREAT SORROW. NOT HURT KEEP HIM WARM. THIS CANNOT BE ENDING OF ALL. ENDING OF ALL. ENDING OF ALL. ENDING OF ALL. MASAR.'

The radio contact had started about 7:30 p.m. and continued until late in the night. We had set up a small refracting telescope in Mr. R's backyard. While observing the Moon we were amazed to see what appeared to be a star just above its outer surface. But it was too brilliant to be a star and it moved in a clockwise direction with the Moon. We observed this object for several hours. Its movements were strange and we wondered if this was some gigantic powerhouse of a space ship relaying our messages from Masar and Jupiter.

At last we would meet our space friends face-to-face. We could hardly believe that we were to be so honored.

28 September 1952

Unfortunately, our plans were poorly made. Our contacts had told us to be careful and plan wisely. None of us knew the exact landing site except Mr. R. We thought it would be safer if only one should decide and the others follow him. Before we drove off in two cars, we told Mr. R to stop at any fork in the road where he might turn off. This would avoid separation. He did just that. He turned off the main road, parked and waited for us. But, as our car neared that point, our view was cut off by the passing of two large logging trucks from the mountains. They were traveling very fast and there was much dust. We spent the rest of the day trying to find each other. Of course, we missed the appointment for 2:00 p.m. We finally found Mr. R and his car back in town about 6:00 p.m. The results of this unfortunate venture made us realize that we were not prepared for such an event. We felt that we had missed the chance of a lifetime ! All of our thinking at that time was directed at the landing contact as an end in itself. We have since realized that Universal service is indeed Eternal! The goals of today become the doorways to tomorrow's duty.

We were all very hungry as Mr. R had the picnic food in his car. After eating we decided we should at least try for radio contact. We didn't think they would ever come in again. Why should they? We had failed them. Yet, we thought perhaps they would give us further instructions. A contact was made about 9:20 p.m. that evening.

'RADIO IS DANGEROUS. YOU MUST NOT USE YOUR RADIO. YOU WILL BE CONTACTED BY A MAN IF OUR PLANS ARE TO BE CHANGED. YES, YES. HOPE THIS SPEED IS COPY. A MAN WILL CONTACT YOU WHEN ALL IS READY. DO NOT USE RADIO. MUST HURRY. OUR TIME IS SHORT. YES YES COPY.'

We waited several minutes before the next code came in.

'END. EU WE LOCATE YOU.'

At 10:45 p.m. another message came in.

'GREETINGS, YOU HAVE — OK. DO NOT EXPUNGE YOUR MINDS. YOU HAVE INHERENT MINDS. USE THEM. WAIT.'

All of these last messages were of short duration with a long pause between each of them. At 11:20 p.m. we again made contact.

'RADIOMAN HAS DEEP SECRET IN HIS MIND. WE WILL NOT REVEAL. WE ARE ALARMED.'

Mr. R turned to us and said, 'If they had known about this before, they would never have picked me for your radioman.' Immediately, they came in again.

'BE OF PEACE.'

Again we waited several minutes.

'HAPPY. HAPPY. YOU RADIOMAN — ARE INSTALLED IN THE RECORDS. GOOD. ATTENTION. SURPRISED MY BROTHER?'

We had no idea what they meant by 'deep secret.' Mr. and Mrs. R knew, however. Nevertheless, we have never been curious enough to ask them what was meant. What they were trying to convey by telling us, 'installed in the records,' we do not know. We received a final message at 1:40 a.m. (29 September 1952). Although much of it was a series of numbers, we copy it here as it was given.

'SR AGFA AWA PERI K-4 K-4 PERI AFFA AGFA ZO PERI. AGFA IS FINISHED. AGFA IS FINISHED. AGFA IS FINISHED. 110 25 AND 900 HA SO 52 AND 90 30 4 02262102 3 33 1500W 252 THE — ON 1002 06000224 2257902072034.'

Even though we had missed a landing with friends from other inhabited worlds, we still had a joyous time in Mr. R's ham shack. Anyone can imagine the suspense, the

73

excitement that all of us felt during these radio contacts. There were usually eight or nine of us huddled together in the little shack waiting for information from our space friends!

30 September 1952 (11:00 p.m.)

It was a wonderful evening to look at the heavens, so we had our small telescope set up in Mr. R's backyard again. A fourteen-year-old neighbor boy came over to join us in our astronomy lesson. We were looking at Jupiter with its bands and some of its twelve moons when this boy said that he had been having strange dreams lately. He said that a voice in his dream told him to tell no one about them, yet while he talked to us he had a strong impression to tell us. The moment he related their details we told him to go into the ham shack and write down everything he could remember.

This young man's name is Ronnie Tucker and he is a student in Winslow, Arizona. His most amazing dream took place the same night that the mind-probe was relayed from Jupiter. After the voice had warned him not to tell anyone of what he saw, he awoke from the dream covered with perspiration and looked out of his window on the porch. He said there was a beam of light about one foot wide, and tubular in shape, misty white, coming from far out in space and going directly into that part of Mr. R's home where his father-in-law was sleeping! Did young Ronnie Tucker see the beam that was conducting the mind-probe on Elder B? He must have, for he knew nothing of our research and couldn't possibly have timed the dream with the Jupiter radio message.

Mr. R wanted to tell the boy about our work, but was afraid to. He told him that there were certain things he should know, but it might take a week or so to decide in his case. The receiving set was turned on to 405 kc. while all this was going on. Immediately the following message came through and Mr. R hadn't transmitted a thing!

'K4 K4 K4 THIS IS K4 K4 K4 THIS IS K4. OK ON THE — K4 K4 OK ON THE NEW ONE. K4 K4 I.'

This was truly wonderful! Our space friends accepted this boy. Now we were certain that, if they wanted to, they could know every thought, action and deed of man on Earth. Ronnie told us that in another dream they told him that they wanted to save our planet. They said they would do all they could with our help. They told him they believed that no man should destroy another but that all men should live Universal Law and love everyone and live in peace, working together. They assured him that life was eternal.

At 6.30 p.m. another board contact was made.

'This in Ankar-22 of Jupiter speaking. Jupiter is the mental research centre of this Solar System. We will continue to help. On your Earth there are magnetic anomalies. Your scientist wonder why meteorites fall in a pattern and in certain locations over the world. They also wonder why great civilizations are found where meteorites are found. The answer is simple. The anomalies attract the meteorites, and these same anomalies amplify Universal influx from outer space. Therefore, you will find better living conditions, finer art and music and so on in the same place you find the meteorites.'

Our space friends had told us that we would be contacted by a man when all was ready. This man undoubtedly would be an inhabitant of another planet. We were most excited over this possibility.

During the month of September 1952, saucers were being seen everywhere by competent observers. The entire world was becoming sky conscious.

During the week of 5 October a cousin of Mr. R's was visiting him in Winslow. This man knew nothing of our research and had never mentioned saucers to Mr. R before. One night the two men were in the radio shack when they suddenly heard a strange low hum and a buzzing sound. Mr. R asked his cousin to go outside and see what it was. 'Come here quickly,' his cousin called. Mr. R arrived too late to see a strange, orange-colored, oval-shaped object hovering directly above his antenna. He said, 'What do you think it was?' His cousin replied, 'That was a flying saucer.' At once they made an attempt to establish radio contact, but it was unsuccessful.

On 12 October at 1:00 p.m. an unusual thing happened. We make mention of it here because so many other people, in dealing with saucer phenomena, have noticed the same thing. We were in Winslow at Al's house, when suddenly we smelled a very powerful odor. It was similar to burning metal in acid. We could not locate its source, and it seemed to be only in the house.

On 21 October at 8:10 p.m., a small private plane crashed and burned at Winslow, Arizona. This plane was on a mercy flight to a Phoenix hospital with a fourteen-months-old polio victim. All four passengers were instantly killed. One of the workers at the Winslow Timber Company was working late, and saw the plane take off and minutes later burst into flames. He told the CAA investigators that immediately after the crash, and before the ambulance and fire truck had arrived, an orange streak sped across the sky and apparently landed by the stricken plane. We know that the saucers do not harm anyone. Perhaps they knew of the child and tried to help. Of course, we do not know just what did take place.

We were now trying to separate our own thoughts from those of the space intelligences. We used the board rarely, for we felt it might be hindering our progress in the development of more direct telepathic contact.

1 November 1952 (6:30 p.m.)

'Artok of Pluto speaking. Have no fright, all is right. Our ships are silver lights; lights of beauty; lights of duty.'

'Ankar-22. Please concentrate, as we are going to go a step ahead in our telepathic work. One of you will receive a message from our brother, Ponnar. Your planet is called Saras because of the repetition of cataclysms that have visited you. Only technical advance has been made on Saras, and this is the wrong kind of achievement for you are now engulfed in darkness that has no equal.'

'Regga speaking. Men of Saras have sought only the ways of the flesh. They have a form of spirituality, but deny the power and majesty of the Creator. The so-called educated man is a fool, the nations are bathed in the blood of myriads of young men, women and children. What will Saras do with her new powers' You are as children with a dangerous toy. We are out in the vastness, and we watch your industries where greed is born; your capitals where wars are born; your laboratories where discoveries are made. We see the birth cradle and we see the early death shroud. There is something far more beautiful, more satisfying, than you have attained. We have been observing you for a long time now. We are your brothers. Have we not shown this to be true over and over again? If there is violence, it will be of your making, not ours! We know that among you there are those who desire and seek the love and knowledge which alone makes man free. We have tasted of it, and it is good, it is sweet. Look up, people of Saras. Be of one mind and purpose. We are not unattainable, for we are here with you! We wait, we watch, we listen!'

Many other messages were received by members of our group by direct telepathic contact, which we never would have received had we not become as one mind. It took weeks of meditation and concentration, holding self down, and allowing ourselves to become attuned to the influx from the Universe.

The Universe has much to offer us if we but stop our senseless wars, and exploitation of our brothers, and return once more to a true realization of Creation. Wonderful and almost unbelievable things await us if we but awaken and arise to meet those who are now awakening throughout the world.

20 November 1952

Mr. and Mrs. Williamson with Mr. and Mrs. Bailey were in company with three other people in the desert near Desert Centre, California, when a cigar-shaped mother ship was observed by all present and a personal contact was made with one of the occupants of a scout-type saucer. [*Flying Saucers Have Landed by* Desmond Leslie and George Adamski.]

Many things happened during December 1952 and January, February 1953. Saucer sightings increased and Nature went on a rampage. We need not go into that here for the newspapers and radio broadcasts covered it thoroughly. However, there were many sightings of great importance that were never heard of by the man in the street.

On 21 December 1952, Mr. R and five other residents of Arizona, observed a large, cigar-shaped mother-craft over the city. They watched it from 5:00 p.m. until dark. Two smaller saucers were seen to enter the larger craft and a few minutes later one left the mother-ship. This was observed through field-glasses.

On 3 February 1953, Mr. and Mrs. Williamson were coming home from town in Prescott, Arizona, when they observed two saucers come within a few feet of the ground. These craft were close enough so that the general outline and the light on top could be observed. There was absolutely no sound. About 10:00 p.m. the same night Mr.

Williamson saw another saucer with an amber light go directly over his house. It was *very* low. Since then many of these space craft have been seen in Northern Arizona and elsewhere. Many people are afraid to tell about what they have seen.

15 February 1953(11:25 p.m.)

We were at Mr. R's for a short conference. We were trying to decided what we should do about this report you are now reading. How should it be written? Should all of the facts be given to the public? We did know that we should continue to be of one mind and then carefully make our plans. We knew, also, that our space friends would want the truth given. Nothing else would do!

Mr. R had the radio set turned on, as he always does when he is in the radio shack. One never knows when a signal might come in from the space craft intelligences. He had transmitted nothing. In fact, he doesn't need to transmit any more. They will answer any and all problems they feel important by coming in on the receiver if it is on. Mr. R also wondered if V (····-) wasn't really EU (· ···-)?

Suddenly a radio code signal just seemed to slide in on 405 kc. At first, Mr. R couldn't make any sense out of the dot and dash system. Finally one word stood out. It was: 'CENTURAS.' We do not know what it could mean except it closely resembles the name of a constellation. Then a very understandable message came through.

'OK THIS TIME IS FOR YOU TO DECIDE. AR. OK OK OK THIS TIME IS FOR YOU TO DECIDE. WE CAN NOT, AK A. AFFA FROM THE P. RA RRR OK K5 K5 FROM THE PLA — CHANG —. RRT IT.'

The message ended at 12:05 a.m., 16 February 1953. They would not decide for us on this report. It was up to us! So, we have set it down exactly as it happened. It is unfortunate that some of the messages were not understandable. Affa was on a ship called K-5, and he was apparently going to give us the name of his own planet and the ship's origin.

We know that all radios in the world are not silent. Many of them are now receiving information from our brothers in the sky! We hope that this report will awaken interest amongst others, and that they will honestly attempt contact with our visitors from space. They have come a long way to help us. Let us extend to them the hand of friendship and welcome!

Please Post in Radio Room and on the Bridge

FOR EARLY WARNING IN DEFENSE OF THE NORTH AMERICAN CONTINENT
MERINT
RADIOTELEGRAPH PROCEDURE

1. WHAT TO REPORT
Report immediately all airborne and waterborne objects which appear to be HOSTILE, SUSPICIOUS or are UNIDENTIFIED.

Surface warships positively identified as not U.S. or Canadian — Guided Missiles

Aircraft or contrails which appear to be directed against the United States, Canada, their territories or possessions

Submarines

Unidentified Flying Objects

2. SEND TO ANY
United States Naval Radio Station
Canadian Naval Radio Stations
United States Coast Guard Radio Station
United States Commercial Radiotelegraph Station
Canadian Department of Transport Coastal Station

Receiving station will relay to military destination

3. HOW TO SEND
* MERINT MERINT MERINT (Coastal Station) DE (Own Signal Letters) K (Own Signal Letters) DE (Coastal Station) K
EMERGENCY (For U.S. or Canadian Naval or Coast Guard Radio Stations)   or
RAPID US GOVT COLLECT (For U.S. Commercial Coastal Stations)   or
RUSH COLLECT (For Canadian Dept of Transport Coastal Stations)

4. SEND TO ONE DESTINATION
ComAirDefForLant Norva
ComWestSeaFron Navy SFran
NavyCharge Halifax
NavyCharge Esquimalt

Select destination nearest to your receiving station

5. SEND THIS KIND OF MESSAGE

Content—	Example—
a. Begin your message with the word "MERINT"	MERINT
b. Give the reporting ship's name and signal letters	SS TOLOA WHDR
c. Describe briefly the objects sighted	TWO UNIDENTIFIED SURFACED SUBMARINES
d. Give ship's position when objects are sighted, also TIME and DATE	5034N 4012W 071430 GMT
e. If objects are airborne, estimate altitude as "low", "medium", "high"	(not applicable)
f. Give direction of travel of sighted objects	HEADING 270 DEGREES
g. Estimate and give speed of sighted objects	15 KNOTS
h. Describe condition of sea and weather	SEA CALM
i. Give other significant information	ELONGATED CONNING TOWERS

6. SEND IMMEDIATELY
a. DO NOT DELAY YOUR REPORT DUE TO LACK OF INFORMATION
b. EVERY EFFORT SHOULD BE MADE TO OBTAIN ACKNOWLEDGMENT FROM RECEIVING STATION THAT MESSAGE HAS BEEN RECEIVED

* The International urgency signal (XXX XXX XXX) may be used as an alternate to clear circuit.

Authorized by Secretary of the Navy

OPNAV 94-P-20

7 THE MAN IN THE MOON

Men of other worlds have beaten us to our own satellite, and have established bases there. This is the reason why we have seen strange lights and blinkings on the moon for many years now. These have never been adequately explained.

These lights on the Moon have been reported by reputable astronomers over a long period of time. The following has been observed:

Star-like lights in the Crater Aristarchus; a pyramid in the open space of Linne; an 'X' visible in the Crater Eratosthenes; a strange symbol visible in the Crater Plinus; the letter Gamma in the Crater Littrow; a luminous cable drawn across the Crater Eudoxus in the Northwest Quadrant of the Moon; strange happenings in the Crater Proclus; and in the Crater Picard. Many strange illuminations have been sighted in the Northwest Quarter of Quadrant of the Moon.

At a distance, the space craft do look like stars. The reason: they operate in a magnetic field just as *all* celestial bodies do! Flow long they have been on the Moon we do not know, but we can be certain that they have used it as a base ever since they began coming to Earth. We have not had telescopes very long, but as soon as this instrument was utilized we saw strange things on our satellite! The 'man in the moon' made us laugh once, but he's an actuality after all! For several months now, we have been receiving letters from all over the United States, Canada, Mexico, England and other countries. Many of these have been from scientific groups and individuals. Several well-known astronomers have told us in writing that they firmly believe the saucer phenomena to be interplanetary in origin. We have these letters on file.

8 SAUCERS STILL SPEAKING

Many groups are now experimenting in radio, trying to contact the saucers. Some of these groups have had success. Others have received nothing and others have not received anything from the saucers themselves over their radio receivers, but saucer sightings have coincided with their transmissions.

We have had more personal contact recently with the saucers, but this is of such a nature that we cannot put it into print just now.

One group, working with radio communication in Ohio has had success in contacting the discs. We have been in touch with them by letter.

A gentleman in Virginia writes the following; 'You asked me to describe the strange speech that came over my FM radio set. My wife and I heard it the first time, but a whole crowd of us heard it the last time, and special effort was made to get some intelligible word out of the conversation which seemed to be between a man and a woman. The first time I found the signal at 98 mc. on 15 April 1952. It was repeated the next day at the same time: 4:15 to 5:25 p.m. EST. The signal was *very* powerful, as indicated by the electric eye, but the voices were low in volume, as if our radio receivers were not precisely designed for the type of modulation being used. The sounds were of even tone like chanting, as if two trumpets were speaking, one low pitch, and the other high pitch, like a man and a woman.

'But the sounds were divided into words and sentences, one, then the other speaking. There wasn't a single word in English. On 16 April 1952 I photographed a huge cloud circle in the sky of this region. It was not caused by jet vapor trails. That same night the enormous vapor trails over Alaska caused the military alert, and the communication line between Alaska and the United States went dead. Also that same day, astronomers observed a double cloud on Mars that rose nearly 100 miles above the surface of the planet. Nothing like it has ever been seen before!

'The next radio voice came on 16 March 1953. It was the same chanting speech, but one of our listeners said he heard the word 'Washington.' This was the only understandable word. Of course, this word would be the same no matter where used. I think this was on 103 mc. Unfortunately, I have mislaid my notes. It was also in the evening. I made some tests this time, and found the signal to come from a certain direction, *straight to the radio, not* through the aerial. When I stood or placed my hand in a certain place, the signal would dim and static would come in. Evidently this message just happened to affect the F M set on that particular frequency.'

On 29 January 1950 in Spain, several radio owners reported strange speech reception while saucers were being observed flying over the country. This was just about a month before the Great Saucer Armada arrival over Farmington, New Mexico. Other saucer sightings were seen at this time. It will be remembered that most of our own communication was done in the months when saucers were being seen everywhere.

In Iowa, there is a very fine group working with radio. It includes prominent professional men and several radio operators. On 18 March 1953 (this almost came on the 16 March 1953 date of the Virginia observations) the following happened to one of the members of this group.

'I was driving from—, Iowa westward. It was about 12:45 a.m. I noticed that on 550 kc. on the radio a very strong code sending was going on. It was a very foggy night and raining. The code became very loud and then would fade away at intervals. I stopped at the top of several high hills to see if I could see anything, but no luck. Finally at one point the fog thinned out and I saw a huge round glow coming down through the fog towards me. It became larger and larger with a bluish-purple color. Suddenly the fog broke away and to the east of the road I was standing on there shone a bright red light, then it turned to white, then back to red again. After changing several times, the fog closed in again and the light appeared as the purplish glow once more. I felt I was being watched! I drove on to —, Iowa after the fog became thicker. The code sending continued and seemed to follow me all the way to town. I dug my partner out of bed at 2:30 a.m. and at his house among large trees the purplish glow came down through the fog again as he and his wife watched. The code signals kept coming in very strong for an hour, finally faded some, so we went to bed at 4:00 a.m. still able to hear the signals, however.'

Several times, immediately after this group would try radio communications, members would sight flying saucers over their town. And since they have been in contact via radio many sightings have been made in that part of Iowa. One time in their messages there was mention of a Bible passage and another time they received: 'WE FIND FEW NOW READY!' This speaks for itself.

Some groups have proven the telepathy part of the radio experiment by receiving messages pertaining to something they had never transmitted to the discs.

Sightings are still being made all over the world, but there seems to be a lull at this time compared with sightings made in the Fall of other years when usually there is a great deal of activity.

However, the saucers are still here and have very important plans for Earth. There will be more catastrophe in the future. The Ionian Island disaster by earthquake off Greece recently is very significant. Our fault lines are under great stress and are giving at certain points. Those Islands are directly over the area where three main, very large fault lines converge! Also, about that time an enormous exploding light was viewed in Denmark.

Yes, the Saucers Are Still Speaking! Let's listen to what they have to say!

9 EPILOGUE (TO ORIGINAL EDITION)

'Yet so shall it be; these fruitless strifes, these ruinous wars shall pass away, and the Most Great Peace shall come.'—Baha'u'llah.

As we complete this report, we watch the newspaper headlines and listen to the newscasts with great interest.

Fantastic Sky 'Spook' Sighted Over Dallas; Navy Gives Chase *(San Diego Evening Tribune. 6* January 1953).

U. S. Jets Chase Saucers Towards Siberia—Radar Picks Up 'Saucers' Over Japan; Pursuit Fails. *(Los Angeles Examiner,* 22 January 1953).

Weird Lights Fly Near Kurile Isles—Air Force Reports Observations By Pilots, Radar Over North Japan. *(Phoenix Gazette,* 21 January 1953).

Pilot Sees 'Disc' Make Pass At Jet. *(Phoenix Gazette,* 27 January 1953).

Jet Chases 'Saucer' At Beach. *(Los Angeles Examiner,* 30 January 1953).

Marine Flier Chases Disc Over Southland—Jet Fighter Unable to Overtake Object; Four Others Reported. *(Los Angeles Times,* 30 January 1953).

Pilot Sights 'Saucers'; Fiery Disc Races Jet. *(Phoenix Gazette,* 30 January 1953).

We could go on and on with newspaper stories and the reports of fearless commentators. The predictions made by our friendly communicators are coming true daily. They have told us that we would see more and more of them in the near future. They said they could not stand by and see another waste. Many of the people of Earth shall see them and no longer doubt who or what they are. *They come as our friends to aid us in a dark hour on this planet.* Soon, we believe, they may even land in great numbers. But this is not an invasion of our world. Billions of Earths were created for mankind. They need not take any one of them by aggressive action.

Let us look up and watch our skies, for our atomic blasts have alerted the Universe, and the flying saucers are here to stay! There are those who hope they will go away, but they never will!

For centuries scientists have set up theories which are guesses based on carefully observed facts. When a few of these scientists want to leave the Desert of Past Mistakes and Guesses, they are held back by the Giant known as Orthodox Science. This Giant has many followers, who claim him to be All Perfection. In the fifteenth century his mighty voice rang out to men like Columbus, 'Thou shalt not believe the Earth is round!' Today he stands there still, shouting, 'Thou shalt not see nor believe in flying saucers.'

There are many well-known scientists today who are devoted slaves of this Giant. They are presumably dedicated to bringing the light to all mankind, yet they hold aloft their own puny torch, hoping someone will carry it on. But its light is dim and flickering. Soon a greater light shall take its place. While the Giant gleefully watches in the darkness, others slip past him into a new day of greater knowledge.

The renowned astrophysicist, Dr. Donald H. Menzel of Harvard Observatory, has written a book that is supposed to tell the whole truth and nothing but the truth about flying saucers. Other scientists have said his laboratory experiments cannot be duplicated in nature. University students who flock to his lectures conic away very disappointed. They say, 'We couldn't help but feel that Dr. Menzel was covering up and leaving something out. It's that "something" that has us worried!'

While Menzel was playing with his car headlights, another world-famous astronomer, Dr. Clyde Tombaugh, discoverer of the planet Pluto, was seeing a space ship! In the sky over Las Cruces, New Mexico, in the summer of 1948, whizzing silently overhead from south to north, was an oval-shaped object. It had about a dozen windows which were clearly visible at the front and along the side. The rear trailed off into a shapeless luminescence. It was traveling too fast for a plane and too slow for a meteor. Many have said that no astronomer of repute has reported seeing unidentified aerial phenomena. However, as we can see from Dr. Tombaugh's report, they are wrong in their statements.

Other so-called authorities were seeing swarms of giant locusts crossing the moon. The same authorities claimed the moon was without atmosphere! Locusts in a vacuum! While they were seeing reflected light on floating dandelion seeds; spiders riding gossamer wisps in the sun's eye; 'flitting flies'; and extra-terrestrial flying barnyards; other scientists with vision, who are also men of science, were seeing the saucers as they really are—spacecraft!

Even stodgy *Harper's Magazine* succumbed to commercialism. They enticed their readers into buying a recent issue by placing the title, 'Little Men and Flying Saucers,' on the cover page. The article, by Dr. Loren C. Eiseley, professor of anthropology at the University of Pennsylvania drags the reader through tales of mermaids, griffins, salamandrine beasts of the coal swamps, carnival freaks, and Darwinism. Very little, if anything, is said about the flying saucers. For a man who is presumably a trained observer, this is indeed a poor observation. He tries to bring in material that has no bearing on the saucer phenomena in order to disprove it. Why? Because he and his cohort, the Giant, have said. 'Thou shalt not!'

He tells us that it is just conceivable that there may be nowhere in space a mind superior to our own! According to him the human ego likes to believe that other worlds are inhabited. And since he is so fortunate in knowing what the truth is, he tells us that man is a solitary and peculiar development on the planet Earth! While others are going forward he is still back in the middle of the desert with Charles Darwin.

Is it egotistical to believe that men are to be found everywhere in the Universe? Or is it egotistical to believe that only the Earth is inhabited—thus making the Earth unique, Does man *want* to be alone on this globe with his many wars, crimes and waste? If he contemplates other inhabited worlds for a moment he sees visions of greater Powers that he may have to answer to.

Some scientists claim that the statistical probability of the life on this planet being reduplicated on another planet is so small as to be meaningless. Yet, the law of averages tells us differently! Dr. Harold C. Urey, Nobel prize-winning atomic scientist, tells us that one quadrillion worlds may originate and sustain life. If we think in terms of Infinity there must be many, many more also.

Certain authorities accept the idea that cellular life may exist out yonder in the dark. But high or low in nature, they do not believe it will wear the shape of man. These same men tell us we are the only thinking mammals on the planet, perhaps the only thinking animals in the entire sidereal Universe. My, my, the burden of consciousness has certainly grown heavy upon us, and it is thus we torture ourselves! These men are all alone in the Creation with their super-brains !

Anyone really studying and knowing animal life would never say that we are the only thinking mammals on the planet.

Getting back to *Harper's* contribution to saucer research again, we find the article tells us that the describers of two-foot men forget that a normal human brain cannot function with a capacity, at the very minimum, of less than about 900 cubic centimeters of capacity. We say that the author of this article has forgotten it is a relative matter! He mentions 'meteors whispering greenly overhead.' There are scientists today who would tell him that meteors are never green!

We are told that nowhere in all space or on a thousand worlds will there be men to share our loneliness. So, there may be boneless, watery, pulpy masses, but of men elsewhere, and beyond, there will be none for ever!

The great scientists of Columbus' time told him that horrible monsters would swallow him and his little ships. Others are telling us the same thing today—that there may be monsters in outer space, but no men! Remember, Columbus found only more men—so will we!

Scientists who really want to leave this dry desert will do just that. All others can stay behind tortured by their terrific burden of a super-brain and their loneliness.

We are told that Dr. Eiseley has been wandering around getting himself covered with sand burrs and other prickly seeds, all of this activity being pertinent to the writings of a book. The prickly seeds must have gotten in his eyes, for if they had been airborne he might have seen a flying saucer. He claims he would rather have lunch with a purple polyp than with a man from Mars. Perhaps he will get his wish!

There is still another type of Giant worshipper that uses the cloak of spirituality and religion. Orthodox science or orthodox religion is the same thing. They are both demanding and dogmatic. This type of man is usually uneducated, for if he were educated he would probably be a super-scientist. Instead, he has no choice but to be a super-religionist. A man-made evangelist bringing hellfire and damnation to all sinners. This type is egotistical and dogmatic.

One of these is Mr. William C. Lamb of Wyoming. He claims he has photographs of God and the Holy City. He quotes reams of Scripture to prove his own opinions. Yet, he believes that atomic energy was a gift of God to his 'angelic Earth children' so that they might blow up all the devils and imps, sending them to everlasting fire and brimstone. This type does not realize that God cannot be photographed. (Even their Bible will tell them so.) The Creator is the unmeasured and timeless one!

We do not believe that a loving God would give man a gift whereby he could destroy innocent women and children in a horrible holocaust! Our Mr. Lamb has astronomical photographs of the Orion Nebula. (Interpreted by him, of course.) God's Throne is supposed to be there. He is telling us that the Creator is smaller and more insignificant than His own Creation! He says the Omnipotence and Omniscience of Deity is a secret that no man is able to fathom, yet he claims to know more about the flying saucers than anyone else. He is contradictory, but fortunately his type is easily discerned. There isn't enough intelligence amongst them to dupe us with lengthy scientific language.

To all of this, we say what Charles Fort said, 'The *trash* that is clogging an epoch *must* be cleared away!'

We see a vision of the future. A world without a slave, man at last free, where our loyalty is not to something called mine, but to all humanity, to the ideal of a higher Universal civilization which will spew out war forever as the vilest of all human defilements. There will be no imaginary boundary lines of nationality, race, color or creed. The Earth will be swept clean of these false walls that for centuries have shut man from man, nation from nation, and have filled the Earth with lamentation and tears, with rivalry and hate, cruelty and oppression, injustice and greed, selfishness and pride, bloodshed, battlefields, and death.

It will be a new world where work and worth go hand in hand, where men's lips are rich with love and truth. A race will exist without disease of flesh or brain, for health will come to all as a divine heritage. And above it all will be the Eternal Father.

Those who cling to the old methods and beliefs will go down with the old order. This is the uncovering period. Soon man will feel deeply that he is indeed his brother's keeper!

Our only remedy for saving ourselves is to turn from hate and national enmity to love and a realization of the Fatherhood of God, the Motherhood of Nature, and the Brotherhood of Man.

10 APPENDIX

We would like to let you know what some of the world's experts are saying.

Brig. Gen. Ernest Moore, former Chief, Air Force Intelligence:

'First off, the Russians have nothing to do with these so-called "saucers"; I'll swear to that on a stack of Bibles, if you like. Second, we don't have any secret new types of aircraft that could have started all this commotion.'

The theory that the saucers were hostile aircraft was carefully studied and rejected. As one scientist said, 'The performance of these "saucers" not only surpass the development of present science but the development of present fiction-science writers.'

As of 25 August 1952, Captain Ruppelt, Air Force, said more competent observers than ever before have been reporting saucers. The Captain, who started as a one-man agency, now has eight fulltime assistants. The Air Force is buying a hundred special cameras, which it hopes will help determine what the objects are made of, and it is considering buying several photographic telescopes of a new type, costing as much as five thousand dollars a piece, with which a continuous photographic record can be made nightly of the sky over the whole hemisphere. After several years and nearly two thousand reported sightings of a serious nature, there is no discussion in Air Force circles of abandoning the pursuit of the elusive saucers.

Twenty-five per cent of the observers interrogated by the Aerial Phenomena Officer in the last few years have been military pilots. Eight per cent have been commercial pilots, some with as much as twenty years' experience in the air, and at one stage in the current phase of the investigation, even a few physicists at Los Alamos, New Mexico, men who make a fetish of objectivity, were interviewed after they reported having seen puzzling lights hovering above their atomic energy laboratories.

On 21 July 1952, Senior Air Traffic Controller for the Civil Aeronautics Administration at the National Airport's Air Route Traffic Control Centre, in Washington, DC, informed the Air Force, and the public that early that morning his radarscope had picked up ten unidentifiable objects flying over various parts of the capital, including the prohibited area around the White House. Controller Harry G. Barnes said, 'There is no other conclusion I can reach but that for six hours on the morning of the twentieth of July there were at least ten unidentifiable objects moving above Washington. They were not ordinary aircraft. Nor, in my opinion, could any natural phenomena account for these spots on our radar. Neither shooting stars, electrical disturbances, nor clouds could, either.

Exactly what they are, I don't know. Now you know as much about them as I do. And your guess is as good as mine.'

On 6 August 1952, an Army physicist at Fort Belvoir, Virginia, created an effect similar to flying saucers in his laboratory by introducing molecules of ionized air into a partial vacuum in a bell jar, and three days later an internationally known authority on atmospheric conditions said of the physicist's experiment, 'I know of no conditions of the Earth's atmosphere, high or low, which would duplicate those needed to make the laboratory models.'

Dr. Fitts and other Project Saucer scientists, said, 'Some of the sightings might be blamed on *muscae volitantes* (flitting flies), the medical term for small solid particles that float about in the field of the eye, casting a shadow on the retina and moving as the eye moves.'

Dr. George Valley, a nuclear physicist at the Massachusetts Institute of Technology; staff members of the research firm of Hand Corporation; an assortment of physicists and aerodynamicists who specialize in the study of the stratosphere and the space beyond it; and the electronics experts attached to the Cambridge Field Station were all searching for physical rather than psychological explanations, and some fairly strange theories occurred to them—the possibility that extra-terrestrial animals were flying into our atmosphere, for example. However, no data turned up to support this arresting idea!

The astronomers concluded that the atmosphere of Venus was composed largely of carbon dioxide and immense, opaque clouds of formaldehyde droplets, and this precluded the practice of astronomy, and hence the concept of a Universe and the idea of space ships.

We feel that perhaps the people of Venus would develop better telescopes than we because of the above conditions, and would therefore have finer equipment than we for viewing the heavens. That cloud layer might excite their curiosity to find out what was beyond it!

There are other theories about Venus, however. John Robinson, in *The Universe We Live In,* tells us that the dust-bowl theory is based on the spectroscopic examination of the upper atmosphere of Venus which reveals no water vapor and quantities of carbon monoxide at that level. He points out that seventy miles above the surface of the Earth the atmosphere contains no oxygen or water vapor at all, and that the atmosphere is almost 100 per cent hydrogen, an entirely unbreathable and highly inflammable gas.

The Earth nevertheless teems with life despite the fact that there is no oxygen or water vapor in the outer four hundred miles of its atmosphere. All oxygen, water vapor and hence life, exist only within a few miles of the surface. This man is not afraid to come to grips with the most modern theories and he searchingly analyzes them.

Months ago our space friends told us that the moon had an atmosphere. The other day, Dr. Harlow Shapley, astronomer at Harvard College Observatory, announced that the moon does indeed, have an atmosphere!

Fred Hoyle, British astronomer, says, 'I think that all our present guesses are likely to prove but a very pale shadow of the real thing.'

Dr. Lincoln La Paz, University of New Mexico, claims that the saucers are not meteors, because they do not look like meteors. He says that fireballs are not shooting stars or meteorites, because meteorites glow for only short periods and invariably make loud noises, while the fireballs and saucers are silent. These objects, he says, can reverse direction and cruise back and forth, travel at high speeds in wide, sweeping circles, are spherical or disc-shaped, give off a steady yellow light for the most part, and travel at extremely high altitudes. Also, meteors are never green in color.

The saucers are not balloons. Mr. J. J. C. Kaliszewski, a supervisor of balloon manufacture, says, 'The saucers are strange, terrifically fast. They have a peculiar glow. One seemed to have a halo around it, with a dark under-surface. We see no vapor trail.'

Dr. Albert Einstein on *23 July 1952,* said, 'Those people have seen *something.* What it is I do not know and I am not curious to know.'

Father Francis J. Connell, C.Sc.R., dean of the Catholic University's School of Sacred Theology said, 'It is well for Catholics to know that the principles of their faith are entirely reconcilable with even the most astounding possibilities regarding life on other planets... Theologians have never dared to limit the omnipotence of God to the creation of the world we know.' He added, 'If these supposed rational beings should possess the immortality of body once enjoyed by Adam and Eve, it would be foolish for our superjet or rocket pilots to try to shoot them. They would be unkillable.'

Anatol J. Schneider, seismologist, stated on 10 June 1946, in San Francisco, that there was great danger of cracking the Earth's surface with atomic bombing by the danger of climate changes occurring throughout the world. It was the underwater bombing that was to be the most feared.

The hands of the clock on the cover of the Bulletin of the Atomic Scientists now stand at three minutes to midnight. When the Bulletin began, the cover pictured a clock with the hands at eight minutes to midnight. The hands are moving up! The hands reflect the feeling of many scientists that since 1945 the world has moved closer to the catastrophe of atomic warfare—that it has become increasingly urgent that we find a solution to the problem of the peaceful utilization of the work of science for the benefit of all mankind.

The world is now close to the Midnight Hour!

11 MR. R'S SECRET

This chapter is dedicated to the memory of the young radioman, who in 1952 made contact with intelligences from outer space via radiotelegraphy and radiotelephony.

Not wishing to disclose his identity, I called him simply: Mr. R (for 'radio'). In the years ahead of us, when history speaks of the turbulent Twentieth Century on Earth, and when all war, disease, greed and selfishness have become nebulous things of ancient legend, Mr. R will be remembered as a pioneer of the days when Earthman learned that he was not alone in the Universe.

Mr. R was the first radio operator to become a channel between the small planet we call home and the vastness of interstellar space. He became a bridge for men of goodwill throughout the Father's limitless realm.

Now his key is silent... for he has graduated to another dimension of time and space. He is now free of the restrictions of Earth, free to communicate forever with worlds without number.

We say, Good-bye, for just a little while, Mr. R... Light ... Love... Peace... as you travel the Great Path up to the stars!

After the highly successful radio experiments of 1952-53, our group decided to write a book on our experiences. We realized that the information we had received was of the greatest importance to all mankind. We asked Mr. R if he cared to write a book about his radio contacts with Outer Space, but he said that he was not interested in making his experiments known publicly, but he did not object if others wrote about them. At that time we had him sign an affidavit, subscribed and sworn to before Genevieve D. Scott, Notary Public, Winslow, Arizona, on the 7th day of March 1953. While he was willing to sign the affidavit, he also told us that he didn't want his name or call letters (since he was a licensed ham radio operator) used in any way whatsoever. This was a great disappointment to us, because we felt that without such information any book on the results of the experiments would fall far short of that which we desired for it. The book would lack the authority that we wanted and needed. However, he was a good friend and we told him we would never disclose his name. We are doing so now in this edition since Mr. R passed away on 23 April 1955, with what was said to be a heart condition and 'other contributing factors.'

The Frontispiece of this book contains the original affidavit revealing the names of Mr. R, licensed commercial and amateur radio operator, and his wife, Mrs. R, plus the name of the Arizona city in which they made their home. Mr. R was Lyman H. Streeter, radio operator for the Santa Fe Railroad. His amateur call letters were : W$_{70}$JQ. He lived at 423 East Maple Street in Winslow, Arizona.

Lyman had good reasons for not wanting his identity known. First of all, he had never used his call letters during his communication with the space intelligences and he never logged any of his receptions. If these facts were made known, he knew he would lose his license, and this was the very last thing he wanted, for to him radio was his *very* life. Also, he knew that even if he had complied fully with the regulations of the Federal Communications Commission, his license would still be taken *away,* for no operator is permitted to make contact with an unlicensed operator and the UFOs aren't licensed with the FCC!

Lyman Streeter's first contact with intelligence from outer space took place the evening of 22 August 1952. He was a good radio operator holding both a commercial and a ham or amateur license. Lyman was very skeptical of the existence of flying saucers let alone the possibility of communicating with such objects by radio. However, he was willing to attempt contact.

Friday evening 22 August 1952, Lyman saw what he thought was a very small meteor display over Winslow. Then he observed what appeared to be a very bright light traveling at a high altitude in the sky directly above him. He turned on his receiver in his ham shack to 400 kc., and immediately, many strange signals were heard but not identified. Later on, the same evening, the Streeters and other witnesses heard strange, clear code signals coming to them as they sat in the main house. Lyman had his ham shack on the back of their property, and he had no transmitting or receiving equipment whatsoever in the main house.

At first, everyone thought the signals were coming from the radio shack in the back yard, but when they went to check, there was absolutely nothing to be heard there... in fact, the equipment wasn't even turned on. After they came back to the main house the mysterious code was heard again. It seemed to be coming from the very air itself. Since that memorable evening in 1952, many others have reported experiencing exactly the same thing.

About 2:00 a.m., 23 August 1952, code signals were again received. Lyman said it sounded as though two people were talking back and forth to each other, using code... but a code unfamiliar to him. It was definitely not standard International Morse Code. The code was coming over his receiver in loud, clear tones. Suddenly, he wrote down a word or two on his note pad; ZO and AFFA.

Later we learned that a superior of Lyman Streeter's in the radio work of the Santa Fe Railroad, a man high up in radio circles, had told him that he also had received strange signals at various times during his radio experiments and that he definitely believed such signals to be from space intelligences. However, he had been evasive when Lyman asked for further information and had seemed to want to discourage him in his own experiments. Why?

One day, this superior called Lyman and told him that Lowell Observatory on Mars Hill in Flagstaff, Arizona had observed UFOs on Friday 22 August 1952. Exactly the same day that Streeter received his first radio signals from space intelligences! This superior also said that a staff member at Lowell Observatory had reported to him earlier that on 22 August 1952, they would focus their large telescope for terrestrial observation over Winslow. But the man had not said what they were going to look for or why. Also, no mention had been made of the source of the information that caused this observation to be made in the first place.

Later, Lyman Streeter had to go to Mars Hill overlooking Flagstaff, where he was making a survey for the Santa Fe Railroad in connection with new radio equipment being installed on the top of Mt. Elden. In an area away from the big observatory, he saw a strange small building surrounded by a high wire fence. Inside the enclosed area he saw two gigantic dogs, obviously watchdogs. Navy men were moving various types of electronic equipment in and out of the little building, which looked new and recently painted. He wondered what such equipment was doing on Mars Hill. He was informed that if the new equipment belonging to the railroad being installed on Mt. Elden interfered with the government work on Mars Hill, then it would have to be placed elsewhere.

Several years later we learned that the government had placed electronic equipment at Lowell Observatory to assist in the tracking of two artificial satellites or space stations that were known to be circling the Earth at four hundred and at six hundred miles out in space. In August 1954, the magazine *Aviation Week* reported that the two objects were *meteors,* and insisted that Dr. Lincoln La Paz of the University of New Mexico had helped in the identification of them as *natural* rather than man-made objects. Dr. La Paz attacked the magazine's reference to him, but acknowledged the search for nearby satellites. He also said: 'The report is false in every particular insofar as reference to me is concerned.' Dr. La Paz and Dr. Clyde Tombaugh, discoverer of the planet Pluto, both worked on the Government project at Lowell Observatory, and both of these men are fully aware that the objects tracked by electronic equipment are not natural, and because of their actions in the heavens could only be artificial... constructed by other intelligent beings. When Sir Edward Appleton, famous British radio physicist, said 'These two unknown objects are discoveries of great astronomical Interest'... he didn't know the half of it. Or did he? It is very likely that Sir Edward knew what La Paz and Tombaugh knew, and the same thing that the United States Government knew when it had the Navy set up an experimental station on Mars Hill. Lyman Streeter stumbled into that secret project in 1952 when he was at Lowell Observatory. Other messages were received, over a period of several months, by Lyman Streeter in his ham shack at the back of the lot at 423 East Maple Street. He had been very skeptical at first. However, after he saw discs in the sky where his radio messages told him to look, discs over his own radio antenna, and after messages were received telling about things which no one but he could have known, and finally, messages coming over the receiver that were answers to questions that had never been transmitted to the intelligences in the usual manner,

Streeter's attitude changed. They had either picked up verbal statements made in the ham shack by telepathy and/or by some kind of recording discs. Soon, our Mr. R had his proof. I remember his facial expression on many occasions; he appeared just too bewildered to even think.

Lyman usually transmitted on 40 meters and received on 405 kc. On one occasion he received via radiotelephone (voice) on 92 meters. However, we are certain that frequency has nothing whatsoever to do with it. Space intelligences have stated many times that they can make anything act as a receiver from radio equipment to the human brain.

At first, Streeter told us that he never had had any interest in UFOs before we contacted him to attempt communication with them. However, upon questioning, he later admitted that he had become very much interested in the possibility of Interstellar Communication in 1950 after he read an article on this subject in QST, one of the amateur ham radio magazines. He said that he had attempted some sort of contact at that time on a high frequency and a short wave length. However, the experiment was a failure and he gave it up.

There was always something strange overshadowing the life of Mr. R that I find impossible to describe in words. The only clue I might have would be a radio message from the UFOs we received during the evening of 28 September 1952. At 11:20 p.m. the following message came through the receiver:

'Radioman has deep secret in his mind. We will not reveal. We are alarmed.'

Streeter turned to the rest of us in the ham shack and said, 'If they (the UFOs) had known about this before, they would never have picked me for your radioman.'

Immediately, code came through the receiver again : 'Be of peace!'

We waited for several minutes without talking until more code started.

'Happy, happy! You, Radioman Kanet are installed in the records. Good! Attention! Surprised, my brother?'

What was meant by 'deep secret'? Evidently Lyman and his wife knew for they looked at each other in a strange way and she came over to sit beside him and hold his hand. Lyman seemed very concerned over this message. None of us was impolite enough to ask the Streeters what it all meant, so we said nothing. Anyway, the space intelligences didn't stay alarmed for long for they spoke of Streeter being 'installed in the records' and called him by another name: Radioman Kanet! This name was formerly left out of the message because we felt it was something that belonged to Streeter alone and could be of no interest to the public. However, it is well to mention it now for it might be a clue for which we are looking.

I remember how, one evening, Streeter told us, rather reluctantly, it seemed, that after attempting contact in 1950 he had appeared one day at work acting in a very strange manner. He went about his assigned radio tasks in the normal way, but his fellow workers noticed he wouldn't answer them when they spoke to him and behaved as if he were in a trance of some kind. His wife was called, and he was taken home. For eight days he was in this unusual 'zombie' condition. He said nothing to anyone during that period. Later, when he regained a state of normalcy, he admitted he couldn't remember a thing that had transpired during those eight days of amnesia.

After the contacts started on 22 August 1952, Streeter suddenly remembered what had happened several years previously (during the memory lapse). He told us that he apparently had left his earthly body (that would account for the zombie condition... the physical body had gone about its usual tasks at work under the direction of the animal mind, while the entity had been elsewhere) and awoke in a beautiful, large hall where many people were gathering. He was called before a tribunal and noticed that he was dressed in fine garments. He was called by a different name (Kanet?)—and told that he must work rapidly to complete his task upon the Earth planet. All he could remember from this eight day journey was the fact that he must work quickly.

His wife said that before the period of amnesia Lyman was just an ordinary radioman, but after his recovery he spent long hours studying electronics and would work for hours on end until he became a top-grade operator.

Besides working at the Santa Fe radio shop, he had his amateur equipment in his ham shack back of his home on Maple Street, and at the other end of this shack his workshop, where he repaired most of the radios, TV sets, recorders, etc., of the neighborhood, including the car radios of the local Police Department. (I remember that once the police interrupted one of our communications with the UFOs by driving into the yard one night and asking Lyman to fix their radio. He obliged, but kept trying to hear the code coming in, listen to the idle talk of the officers and fix the radio, all at the same time.)

Evidently, Lyman H. Streeter was a 'Wanderer'. His name had been Kanet, and he was born on Earth to assist the programme of the Space Confederation. His so-called amnesia experience must have been his awakening period. [See page 206 in the book, *Other Tongues-Other Flesh* (Neville Spearman) —Editor]

On 21 October 1952, something occurred that was to change the life of Mr. R. At 8:10 p.m. a small private plane crashed and burned at the airport at Winslow. This plane was on a mercy flight to a Phoenix hospital with a fourteen-months-old polio victim. All four passengers were instantly killed. One of the workers at the Winslow Timber Company (where Mrs. Streeter also was employed) was working late, and saw the plane take off and minutes later burst into flames. This man told the Civil Aeronautics Administration investigators that immediately after the crash, and before the ambulance and fire truck had arrived, an orange streak sped across the sky and apparently landed by the stricken plane! [UFOs appearing at the moment of birth or death are mentioned in the book : *Road In The Sky,* by George Hunt Williamson (Neville Spearman) -Editor.]

Several days later, a man appeared at the Streeter home and introduced himself as 'Mr. Clark.' He asked Mrs. Streeter for Lyman and was told that he was outside in the radio shack. The man went out and introduced himself to Lyman, saying that although he was not on an official visit, he was with the CAA (Civil Aeronautics Administration) and had just completed his investigations of the crash of 21 October. He showed Lyman his credentials. Then, on a friendlier note, he said:

'I'm a ham operator myself.'

Then he gave his call letters. (Streeter later checked up and found that there was a Clark with the call letters the man had given, but his address was not the same as that which had been given him.)

The visitor then sat down, and said bluntly:

'Streeter, what do you think of the flying saucers?'

Lyman sensed something strange underneath all the apparent friendliness, but he answered honestly:

'I have my own personal opinion, if that's what you mean. I think they come from Outer Space.'

And then, *very* quickly, the man looked Lyman in the eyes and said:

'You've had radio contact with these things, haven't you?'

Streeter realized that this man, Clark, or whoever he was, knew whether he had had radio communication or not, so he said simply:

'I have conducted certain radio experiments under established scientific procedures. Yes, I have had contact with the flying saucers!'

Whereupon Clark asked, 'Would you mind showing me what you received from them? It's no secret is it?'

Streeter reached for his notes in a drawer, as he answered. 'No, it's no secret. I'll be glad to read you what I have, but I must tell you that because the messages were sent so fast, I missed many of the words, so the messages are incomplete.'

Lyman started to read one message after another. Soon he noticed that whenever he came to a blank space, Clark would fill it in! Finally, Streeter said:

'Look here, you must know more about the messages I received than I do!'

'That's right,' Clark answered. *'We monitored everything* you transmitted and received.'

Lyman was startled, to say the least! He said: 'What do you mean by we, the Government?'

Clark hesitated, put his cigarette out, looked intently at Lyman for another moment, and then said:

'Of course, who else?'

Streeter could hardly believe his ears! Confirmation of his experiments at last! But any ideas along this line were soon to be changed rather drastically. Lyman quickly answered:

'You mean to tell me, Mr. Clark, you admit that flying saucers really exist, are coming from Outer Space, and that I have personally had radio communication with these objects?'

Clarke didn't hesitate in his answers:

'Of course I admit it, but you won't be able to prove it to anyone. You see, no one knows I've been here but you and your wife, and besides, I would never admit we talked about such things. I have been in Winslow strictly for the CAA investigation of the recent plane crash. Remember?'

Weakly, Lyman said :

'Just what does your visit to me mean?'

'This is the story,' said Clark. 'About the same time you were receiving your coded messages from the extra-terrestrials, fifteen other ham operators throughout the United States received the same kind of information. We have contacted them all and every one of them is willing to co-operate with his Government. Are you?'

Lyman, still unable to believe what was happening answered:

'What do you mean by *co-operation,* Mr. Clark?'

Then, the CAA man pulled his ace-in-the-hole.

'Look, Streeter, we have you dead to rights. You never used your call letters, you never logged your information, and even if you had done all of that, we still can take away your license because you were in communication with unlicensed operators! The FCC (Federal Communications Commission) frowns on such activity, you know! Now, you don't want to lose your radio privileges—after all, you are commercially licensed besides holding your amateur ticket, you're making, a good living from radio. If your license is taken away, what would you do?'

This was the day Mr. R had been dreading. Many times he had told us that there was the possibility of getting in trouble with the FCC because of the unusual nature of the radio experiments. Clark then started waving the stars and stripes by saying:

'Lyman, your Government is doing all it can to enlighten the people in connection with the coming of the flying saucers. But the time is not ripe yet. A vast educational programme has been planned, and gradually people will come to realize that all space is inhabited, but now the effect would be disastrous if people were to know the truth. Join the other fifteen operators and cooperate with us. We understand your friend Williamson is ready to have a book published called *The Saucers Speak!* and that it deals with the radio contacts. You know about this don't you?'

'Yes,' said Lyman, 'but my name and my city are not mentioned. No one will be able to locate me from the account in the book. My friends have promised to leave me out of it.'

'That's all right,' said Clark, `but the Government doesn't want the radio contact story to be released at this time. You'd better get in contact with Williamson and tell him that the book just can't come out at all, and be firm about it!'

Lyman answered:

'What can I tell him? I've already given him permission to do the story as long as my identity is withheld. He will think it's strange for me to want to stop the book now that it's ready to be distributed!'

'That is your problem, Streeter,' said Clark. 'But the story just can't come out now. Clark went patriotic again, and added: 'Your Government will release such information in due time, but more evidence must be accumulated first. Tell your friend that your job is in danger, and your license. Tell him anything, but stop that book! We can't contact him, for we have his source of information—namely you, as radio operator. Besides, if we talk to him it will only give him proof that the entire affair was authentic. After all, he may still have a few doubts in the back of his mind. Who knows?'

Streeter was almost speechless, as he said:

'What is expected of me?'

'You must co-operate to the limit with us, but I must warn you that we will not be able to back you up or support your story in any way whatsoever if you ever tell your contact story or mention my being here today, or our conversation!'

'In other words,' said Lyman, 'it will be one-sided co-operation?'

'In the interests of national security,' said Clark. 'Yes, it will be strictly one-sided!'

Mr. R had no choice. Although his visitor didn't state it in so many words, it was plain to see that if he didn't co-operate, the FCC regulations would be brought into the picture and he would lose his radio privileges, and, of course, his job with the Santa Fe Railroad! His only answer could have been that which it was:

'What is the first step?'

'We want you to increase your power here for transmitting,' said Clark. 'How soon can you do this and be ready for some experiments?'

'I can't afford to change my equipment now,' said Lyman, 'it would be too expensive!'

'We will send you the necessary parts, Streeter,' Clark said as he rose to go. 'But not a word to anyone, and you'd better not give any more information to Williamson.'

Clark had been sent, not as an official from the FCC, for the Government felt that would be too severe a shock for Mr. R and that he might not give out any information at all. So, they had sent a CAA investigator who was also a ham, knowing full well that there is a comradeship between all radio amateurs, and this was to serve as the tie that binds and so establish communication between Clark and Streeter.

Mr. R received his needed equipment within a few weeks and started to experiment at once, but never again did he receive anything from the space intelligences after his decision to co-operate with the powers that be! Later, he was visited by two officials of the FCC itself who told him to increase his efforts at contact. This he did, thereby affecting many of the neighborhood electronic gadgets, so he stopped. He was attempting to beam all messages straight up in a powerful way that would not be needed in ordinary ham procedures in contacting other amateurs throughout the world. Why he was told to increase his power, I do not know, because while science says that high frequency and high wattage is necessary for any kind of interstellar communication, we know now that *power* is not important, but that the *type wave* used is important.

Streeter called me in Prescott and asked me to stop the book. Since he had already agreed to my writing the book, I thought he was only worried over the risk of his possible identification, and since I felt quite sure that Lyman was completely safe in my presentation, the book could still come out without any harm to him. Later I was to learn that he was concerned over something else.

I had realized for many weeks that Lyman wasn't acting normally. He avoided us, and while he didn't really seem unfriendly, at the same time he was quite cool, as though he knew something that he couldn't tell us. Later we learned that this was true, due to the fact that he had been visited by Clark... who gave his full name as William (Bill) Clark.

We were quite busy with other UFO happenings, however, about this time. Mr. and Mrs. Bailey and my wife and I were on the desert near Desert Centre, California, on zo November 1952, when George Adamski made his memorable contact with a Venusian. Many people have thought that because of our radio contacts we must have arranged that meeting on the desert, but that is not so, for due to Streeter's new commitments, we were not in radio contact at that time. No arrangements were made beforehand by anyone; we simply went out on the desert and what transpired was completely unexpected by all present.

Many other things of interest happened during December 1952, January and February 1953 . UFO sightings increased and nature went on a rampage. On 21 December 1952, Lyman Streeter and five other residents of Arizona, observed a large, cigar-shaped object over Winslow. They watched it from 5:00 p.m. until dark. Two smaller UFOs were seen to enter the larger craft and a few minutes later one left the mother-ship. All of this was observed through binoculars.

On 3 February 1953, my wife and I were coming home from downtown Prescott, Arizona, when we observed two objects, brighter than the planet Venus, which was in a different position in the sky, come within a few feet of the ground. These craft were close enough that the general bell-like outline and the light on top could be easily observed. There was absolutely no sound. I called the US Weather Bureau and was told that there were no planes or balloons in my area. Later the same night I observed another object with an amber light pass very low over my house.

On 15 February 1953 we decided to visit Streeter in Winslow, although at that time we still did not know about his talk with Clark and we didn't understand his coolness towards us. There were several things we felt needed clearing up in regard to the book, which would shortly be released. We hoped the UFOs would have some ideas or advice for us. We told Lyman that we didn't know whether all the facts should be given to the public or not. He had little to say, for he had already told us that he didn't want the report to come out because of the danger to him and his position. He had the radio receiver turned on for he always kept it that way when he was in the ham shack. He transmitted nothing in connection with our request. In fact, he transmitted nothing at all! Suddenly a radio code signal just seemed to slide in on 405 kc. At first, Streeter couldn't make any sense out of the dot and dash system used. Finally, one word stood out: *Centuras.* This was followed by a very understandable message:

'OK. This time it's for you to decide. We cannot.'

The message ended at 12:05 a.m. 16 February 1953. The UFO intelligences would not decide for us. We had to do that! So, in this book I haven't given the account exactly as it happened. We thought perhaps it would have been better to omit the telepathic section of our experiences, for after all it is not untruthful to tell only part of a story! After this communication we felt it best to tell the telepathic experiences as well as the subsequent radio contacts.

Later, Streeter called me again and told me to stop the presses and prevent the publisher from coming out with the book. I thought this a strange request, for already I had assured him that his identity was hidden. But he said:

'I told you I wanted to be protected, and you didn't live up to your promise because now I hear the book is to be released!'

I told him that I had never agreed to stopping the book, but merely to protect him, and added:

'But, Lyman, it will be impossible for anyone to know who you are or where you live. You are completely safe.'

When he still insisted that I stop the book, by force if need be, I became very suspicious, and started an investigation which led to my discovery of the Clark episode. Previously, he had agreed to my writing the book provided that he be left out of it, but suddenly when the book was practically in the hands of the public, he did a quick turnabout. Something was wrong somewhere! I wanted to know what, and I found out. First, one visitor in the form of Clark and then two more men from the FCC. There is little doubt in my mind that Lyman H. Streeter had been visited by the notorious 'three men in black!'

A. David Middelton, who has a wide and varied background in electronics and the communication field decided to investigate Mr. R. Somehow he learned his identity, and personally interviewed Streeter. Middelton is a Senior Member of the Institute of Radio Engineers and was formerly a director of the American Radio Relay League. He holds an Extra Class Amateur License and maintains W 5 CA. Middelton was a project engineer at Fort Monmouth during World War II and also a civilian radar field engineer attached to the U S Navy. Moving to ARRL headquarters, he was Assistant Editor of QST, and later corresponding Editor of CQ magazine. Currently he is working for the United States Government in electronics.

In January 1955, Middelton (W_5CA) discussed the radio contacts with Lyman Streeter in person in Winslow. Later, I provided additional details. 'After full consideration of all data,' said Middelton, 'it is my opinion that these contacts were made by Mr. R as described.'

About the same time, early in 1955, Middelton received reports of radio contact established between UFOs and a VE_3 radio operator in Canada. He stated at the time that he 'believed the contacts were authentic although technical details were lacking.'

The question Middelton asked, and rightly so, was:

'Why have bonafide amateur UFO contact data been conspicuous by their absence in ham discussions on and off the air? Could it be that the amateurs involved have been afraid to report such contacts (Q S O s)? Afraid of what, or whom? Or, maybe there just have not been UFO amateur contacts other than the W_7 and VE_3 experiences!'

Because of Clark's statement about the fifteen other amateur radio operators, we know there were more than W_7 and VE_3. That leaves us with: 'Afraid of what, or whom?'

After examining the facts in regard to Lyman Streeter's contacts, Middelton wrote the following letter:

Federal Communications CommissionAmateur Division, Washington, DC

9 April 1955

Dear O M s,

This is a formal and serious inquiry.

In view of information reaching me from seriously interested sources, the situation might arise wherein an amateur operator, duly licensed and operating within the amateur bands of this country, might be called by a station purporting to be from Outer Space or from Unidentified Flying Objects. Such stations also operating in our bands.

The calls signs used by these U F Os are not any more unusual than many of the strange and weird ones being assigned by some foreign countries, I understand. In view of this fact, it would be difficult to ascertain if the station was, in fact, just another DX country, or one not on this planet, as far as the call sign is concerned.

Will you please inform me as to the feelings and desires of the Amateur Division of the F C C on this matter, if any. Also, will you please inform me of regulations covering this matter?

I realize that this is a strange inquiry but it is definitely in order, and made in a sincere effort to ascertain the FCC views on this matter.

Also, what about amateurs transmitting within our authorized bands but receiving on frequencies outside the bands? This, too, is of concern. This involves Q S Os wherein the amateur did *not* make the call up.

I would appreciate having your reply to this matter, with any degree of secrecy you wish to place on it.

Respectfully yours,

(Signed) A. DAVID MIDDELTON, W$_5$C A

Middelton wanted to ascertain FCC views on the matter, and that is exactly what the FCC didn't want him to do. His high reputation in this field, and the fact that his technical articles have been widely acclaimed in radio circles and reprinted throughout the world, didn't do very much to convince the FCC they could answer him 'with any degree of secrecy' at all! He received a letter from them as follows:

Federal Communications CommissionWashington 25, DC

25 April 1955

File: 7400A. David MiddeltonTijeras, New Mexico

Dear Sir,

This is in reference to your letter of 9 April 1955, requesting comments concerning regulations which would apply to possible communications with unidentified objects.

In regard to amateur radio stations, Section 12.101, of Part 12 of the Commission's Rules Governing Amateur Radio Service specifies the points of communications permitted for amateur stations licensed by the Commission.

Within the limitations of Section 12.101, amateurs may communicate with stations which transmit on frequencies outside the amateur frequency bands.

Very truly yours,

(Signed) MARY JANE MORRIS*Secretary*

Between the time Middelton wrote to the FCC on 9 April, and the time he received an answer from Washington on 25 April. Lyman H. Streeter (Mr. R) had passed away on 23 April.

Needless to say, the extreme mental anxiety and pressure placed upon Lyman

Streeter didn't exactly place him in a state of exuberant health. He was a very young man to die, but I feel certain that 'Kanet,' the radioman, had done his job and had completed the mission he came here to do. Who is to say? Surely not the FCC!

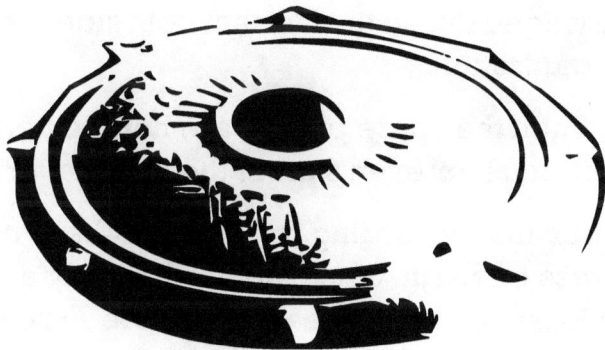

12 COSMIC RAYS AND A BABY SUN

The inevitable question seems to be: 'When and where will the UFOs land on Earth?'

To answer this, it is best to give the statements made by space intelligences themselves. When they were asked what they would do to prevent an atomic war on Earth, they exclaimed: 'We will do absolutely *nothing* to prevent or stop such a war!'

They have stated that they do not know whether there will be such a civilization-destroying war or not. However, they point to the fact that all ancient prophecy, whether found in the Holy Bible, in other sacred books, or in manuscripts, definitely indicates that there will be a conflict of such magnitude that our present civilization will collapse completely.

They have stated in numerous authentic contacts that if we decide on peace and follow a true One World Policy, they will eventually land, share some of their great developments with us, and assist us in taking our rightful place in the Interplanetary Brotherhood. They have further stated that if we do not decide on peace, and an atomic war emerges, they will not interfere but will let such a war progress to the stage where it can no longer be effectively waged due to the fact that both sides have been defeated by the total ruin of technical organization.

Some might ask: 'But if the space people are here to help us, why will they allow such a frightful war to continue, or even start in the first place?'

We must remember that according to Universal Law, our space visitors cannot interfere with our progress on Earth. Since the Earth is only a classroom in the Father's many mansions certain lessons must be learned before Earthman earns graduation to higher spheres. An eighth grader doesn't enter the first grade to make fun of the students because they do things more simply than himself. Likewise, spacemen aren't going to step in and dictate to us; they are going to let us learn our lessons in our own way, even though they will undoubtedly be painful lessons, for the history of the Earth has proven this to be always true on this sorrowful planet!

Space mentors declare, however, that the world is not going to end, even though there will be terrain changes, and violent storms, etc., still man is only to inherit the beautiful and good on Earth. After millennia this planet has managed to produce a harvest of souls who can live in fellowship, love and peace with their fellow men. It is this harvest or remnant that shall inherit the New Earth of the Golden Dawn.

I do not support the prophet of doom predictions that claim our world will be utterly destroyed. But that there will be great destruction *locally* in various parts of the Earth *there is no question!* Yet will it not be worth it, if we awaken to a New Earth, purified and cleansed of all lust, greed and war? Is this not the Great Dream of all ages?

You ask: 'But what about the millions who will perish? Is this not a terrible loss?'

Let us remember that life is eternal... therefore no one will actually perish, they will only leave a planet that is no longer suitable for their development. Those who have not yet learned the lessons contained in the Sermon on the Mount will be reborn on other worlds where they will remain until they learn Universal Laws and how to apply them.

The space intelligences do not look upon death the same way as we do. If we are born to die, then we must also *die* to *live! Why* are the UFOs here? It is a difficult question to answer, but is usually summed up in the following: '

1.   Atomic experiments on Earth and our advancement in eventual space travel and the exploration of space have alerted other inhabited planets. [America expects to land a man on the Moon during 1968—Editor.] (There is always an increase in UFO sightings and fireball phenomena after atomic experiments and the launching of sputniks.)

2.   This is the psychological time for outer space intelligences to make their appearance on Earth due to the above (No. 1) reason.

3.   The space visitors wish to assist the remnant on Earth after catastrophe and return the Earth to the Interplanetary. Brotherhood from which it fell countless generations ago.

4.   They (UFOs) are fulfilling prophecy concerned with the approaching New Age, Great Cycle or Second Coming.

5.   Space friends intend to evacuate large portions of Earth's population in the event the axis of Earth shifts. [*See Inside The Space Ships by* George Adamski.]

Apparently the above reasons sum up the main purposes for the coming of the U F Os. However, for some time, I have been aware that there is a much bigger and even greater purpose be hind it all which the U F Os have not yet revealed in any contacts.

Although they show great love towards us, why have they decided to put in a mass appearance at this time? What arc they educating us for? If we are progressing in our own classroom why should they disturb us at all: What great cosmic change or knowledge of it has prompted them to come now?

At first, the man-in-the-street wants to know if there are, indeed, 'little orange balls going that-away!' Once he is convinced that something is 'going that-away,' then he wants to have the greater answer: *Why* are they?

In some contacts, a great dust cloud has been mentioned, and the fact that our Earth is now in the outer fringes of this area. Undoubtedly, by dust cloud they are referring to a great cosmic cloud or area of intense cosmic ray activity that not only our Earth is entering, but our entire Solar System.

Evidently, for centuries, scientists of other worlds have realized that our Solar System was heading directly for the centre of this cosmically disturbed area, and they knew what would happen when the Earth and its neighbors plunged deeper and deeper into this dark cloud of space! Yes, we are now on the outer fringes of a great field cloud of energy, and are experiencing the first effects in the form of strange weather, melting polar ice caps, earthquakes, increased cosmic ray bombardment and the effect on radio broadcasting. The latter was brought to the public's attention some months ago. The governments of the world have been aware of this change for some time and are deeply concerned. Special projects have been set up to study radiation and its effect on organic life.

'Project Rome' was set up to study the magnetic effects at the North and South Poles. Since a planet is a space ship itself, what better way to investigate the Universal Energy that powers such a craft, than to study the force at its source, the polar events of the Earth itself. Project NQ-707 was organized to attempt communication with the UFOs (at Edwards Air Force Base, California).

During 1955-56 I was in correspondence with a well-known foreign scientist who said that after intensive research by government scientists they came to a terrifying conclusion: *that our planet is moving very rapidly on a collision course with a gigantic embryonic sun!*

Research in this country by men such as Dr. Kurt Sitte, Syracuse University, and Dr. Jason, J. Nassau, Director of Warner-Swasey Observatory, Cleveland, Ohio, and others, shows us that indeed, the electron count has speeded up and the cosmic ray bombardment increased fantastically. The International Science Symposium held recently in Rome reached incredible conclusions.

What does this collision course really mean to the people of the world? First of all, relax, for it very definitely does not mean the end of the world. Eventually, perhaps centuries from now, man will have to leave the Earth, his old home for the last few million years, and migrate through interstellar space to a new home. But for our generation and time we are told we need not be concerned with the world ending. A new Golden Age is about ready to be born on the Earth and the planet beneath our feet will have to be here if we are to reap the glorious benefits of such a New Age. However, as we plunge deeper into the magnetic field of the new baby sun, the effects will become more noticeable, and this will increase as times goes on.

The most closely guarded secret of all time is not that visitors from Outer Space are here on Earth, but *why* they are here. They have come to prepare us for a new technology and age on our world so that we might be ready for the eventual journey through space that defies description. We are gathering data all the time on this and it will be presented as we receive and study it.

Unfortunately, our designated superiors and authorities are not preparing us for anything. It is pretty obvious that politicians aren't going to help us, neither are militarists, scientists nor religionists.

Noted astronomers are certain there is life on Mars. Great areas change from brown to green with the seasons and other blue-green areas change in tint. This is good evidence of vegetation or plant life. But what about more intelligent beings, Astronomers know beyond the shadow of a doubt that an intelligent race of beings exists on Mars because photographs taken during research in 1954 prove the existence of the canals and, more important still, prove that they are artificial, constructed by men like ourselves.

Scientists have had ample time since 1947, when the UFOs were first given widespread publicity, to do an about-face on their lifeless universe theory. They could have saved face by suddenly telling the public that through their great discoveries they had found intelligent life existing on neighboring worlds! No one, in the excitement, would remember that until the announcement was made science had refused to accept such a belief. However, propaganda in the hands of an expert works wonders with the masses. For example, remember how millions of Americans suddenly had their minds changed for them during World War II...'Bloody Joe' (Stalin) became 'Uncle Joe', and we had to learn to love Russia, a country we formerly were told to hate. After World War II, the public had its mind changed, and the allies we needed during the war had to become the hated ones again.

Once man had accepted life outside his own puny Earth, he would have been ready for the greater revelation. Not only is there life out in space, but it is now coming to Earth in the UFOs.

But there have been no statements from the 'priestly' scientists! Will they reveal their discoveries about Mars, the Moon and the other Planets? They will not! Any astronomer who has dared to make a public statement has been literally shut up by having the security curtain dropped over him.

The UFOs are here to help awaken us. 'They are the fulfillment of all ancient prophecy in that they remind us that `our salvation draweth nigh.' The religious leaders of the world and their churches have done practically nothing about informing their flocks of the importance of the coming of the discs. That the UFOs tie in with prophetic statements of the Bible there is no question! What then is the matter with the clergy of the world? They are men of God who are supposed to bring Truth to the hungry sheep of the Lord.

But are they *really* men of God? *By their fruits ye shall know them* the Bible tells us. So, let us examine the fruit of the clergy for a moment. If they and by 'they' we mean any religious leaders of any denomination—really believe in Jesus the Christ and what He taught as Divine teaching, then why do they not interpret His words correctly?

During World War II ministers on both sides exhorted: 'God is on our side, so you young men go out and fight for your country, your freedom and your Creator!' This is simply the pagan idea that God at various times takes sides and allows one group of men to kill and maim another group of men. It is the kind of theology that holds up a bloody god of war and death as the Supreme Intelligence of the Universe, an all-loving God! How contradictory can they become?

God takes no sides! Christ does not, and could not condone any war! Here is a challenge: Let the self-appointed priests of this world tell all men everywhere that because Christ said 'turn your check,' 'meet hate with love,' 'love your enemies,' 'he that takes up the sword will surely die by the sword,' 'do good to them that hate you,' they (they men of Earth) should never take up arms again to destroy their fellowmen.

If the World's great Christian religious leaders would tell mankind that it is utterly and completely against the teachings of Jesus the Christ to fight and kill, do you think a successful war could be waged? What if such an order came from the Vatican? What if a Catholic would suffer ex-communication for becoming a soldier or even for engaging in defense activities? A great number of potential fighting men in the world's population would be lost to the cause of the Hidden Empire wars.

But apparently people believe what they are told, and in many cases they don't want to think; it is much easier to let someone else do that. How many times have we seen paintings of Jesus with outstretched hands bestowing blessings on servicemen girded to the loins with all kinds of devilish devices for taking the life of a brother, another spark of Divine Life?

"The fault may lie at the door of the Emperor Constantine and his conclave of bishops and priests. This ruler in AD 325 assembled at Nicaca in Bithynia, a great council of over three hundred prelates, representing the different Christian churches throughout the Roman Empire and its satellites. They put into binding circulation certain dogmas, creeds and doctrines for the followers of the humble Christ. Therefore, a military emperor put his imperial signature to documents that were to affect most powerfully the destinies of the Christian nations, indeed, the whole world.

A military man cannot suddenly be called to the role of Dove of God or Dove of Peace. Today, the so-called rulers of Earth are nothing but the puppets of the International Cabal. Go to the polls and vote and you don't vote for this man or that, for no matter who is elected, only one power is going to be in control anyway—the same power that has been in control since man came to Earth and knew the difference between good and evil! It is the same power that made Constantine hide his bloody battle armor and act out the role of Christ's representative on Earth.

The Bible and other sacred books have been changed until they are no longer recognizable. Man has been enslaved by the powers of darkness on this strange little planet. But the time is fast approaching—in fact, is it not here? — when men will no longer look to priests and kings, to scientists lost in their own imaginings, to authority wherever it exists! Man has access to the throne of God himself. He needs no one to save him from anything. Do not listen to the mouthpieces of the Hidden Empire, the politicians who promise you this or that for your physical existence, the priests who offer you life everlasting and eternal glory if you follow them, the generals who exist only because of war and suddenly are presented holy before you as god-fearing, righteous men, scientists who promise to give you immortality from a test-tube when you already are an immortal being!

Howbeit in vain do they worship me, teaching for doctrines the commandments of men. (Mark 7: VII).

Those who would place themselves over you as your guardians are teaching you the commandments of men and are passing them off as the doctrines of God! Wake up! In the name of an all-loving and compassionate Creator, *wake up!*

The quicker we realize that this is *revolution,* the quicker the job will be done and the Kingdom of Heaven established upon the Earth. Yes, this is revolution, a revolt against tyranny, greed, lust, war, hatred and opposition to the basic rights of all men. Let us not be found wanting. Stand with your Creator and not with the forces of darkness. If God is with us, who can be against us?

Recently, I heard a well-known radio minister tell his listeners that man was basically a terrestrial being and had no business snooping around in Outer Space. He said that other suns and worlds were God's secrets and man should not attempt to meddle in the Creator's private business. He believes that God will stop man from exploring space by direct intervention. In other words, God hasn't stopped man from committing the most atrocious crimes against Universal Law, but now He is going to step in and prevent us from taking a closer look at His celestial wonders.

What rubbish! Man is *not* essentially a terrestrial being. He is a *spiritual* being that takes physical form so that spirit may come to know itself. How gullible do such ministers think men are? Our ancestors believed that the stars were lights that God set into motion on tracks, and every night sent them around the heavens to amuse His chosen Earth-children. You laugh? And well you might ! But the situation is no better today. We are told that we must believe that all celestial bodies outside of little Earth are strictly taboo. 'Hands off!', says God.

This same type of thinking has existed throughout all ages, and it enslaves mankind. But now the time is at hand when truly our 'salvation draweth nigh.' Man will shortly stand as a true son of God himself, living in *Truth.* The vibrations of the New Age will not permit falsity of any kind to exist on Earth. The old falls away, all is made new.

Look at present world conditions, look at the wars and rumors of wars. Yes, there will be chaos on Earth, but fear not, for out of the tribulation ahead shall come the most beautiful age man has ever known on Earth, the pitiful little 'Red Star.'

Do not be deceived by those appointed over you who are in league with Anti-Christ. Believe no one just because he says it is true; do not even believe this book, but listen only to the dictates of your own heart and soul.

He that shall endure unto the end (of the age), the same shall be saved.

James Russell Lowell said: 'Once to every man and nation, comes the moment to decide...' Perhaps, also only once to every planet comes the moment to decide. This is, indeed, the *moment* to do just that!

Do not be found asleep. Watch, for no man knoweth the hour!

GLOSSARY

ACTAR—From Mercury; Radio Centre of our Solar System.

ADEE—Capital City of Etonya; Jupiter.

ADU—From Hatonn in Andromeda.

AGFA AFFA—From Uranus.

ANKAR-22—From Jupiter.

ARTOK—From Pluto.

AWA—A contact.

BARRAGA—Friends in the Solex Mal.

BELGA—Um's special space craft.

BELL FLIGHT—Flying Saucer Fleet.

BEN—Good in the Solex Mal.

CHAN—The Planet Earth; means 'afflicted' in certain ancient languages.

CLACTEEM—Special ship from Masar for landing contacts.

CREATIVE SPIRIT—God; the Creator.

CRYSTAL BELL—A flying saucer, UFO.

DA—Code for Outer Space Contact.

DEIMIOS—One of the artificial satellites of Mars.

ELALA—Planet 15 of Solar System 22, formerly called Wogog.

ELEX—Young son of Zo and Um.

ETONYA—The Planet Jupiter.

EU—Code symbol for the Planet Earth.

FOWSER—The dark moon, or second moon of Earth.

GARR—From Pluto.

GIN-GWIN—Chippewa Indian word for flying saucer.

HATONN—A planet in the galactic system of Andromeda.

KADAR LACU—Kalar Laqu: Head of the Universal Tribunal on Saturn.

KARAS—A contact.

K - 4—A space ship.

K - 5—A space ship.

LOMEC—From Venus.

MACAS—Neptunian cattle.

MASAR—The Planet Mars.

MORNING STAR—The Planet Venus.

NAH-9—Head of Solar X Group; a contact group from the Planet Neptune.

NORO—Head of a landing contact group.

OARA—Planetary representative of Saturn.

ORION—Universal evil influence emanates from this area in the heavens.

PATRAS—Planet next beyond Pluto in our own Solar System which contains twelve planets altogether.

PHOBOS—One of the artificial satellites of Mars.

PLANET 5—Formerly the planet between Mars and Jupiter, now known as the asteroid belt (Lucifer).

PONNAR—Universal Head from the Planet Hatonn.

REGGA—Planetary representative of Mars.

RO—From the Toresoton Solar System.

R - 3—A space ship.

SAFANIAN—Another Solar System.

SAGAFARIS—Another Solar System.

SARAS—The Planet Earth; in ancient Chaldean it means repetition. (Also, Saros).

SEDAT—Keeper of Records in the Temple of Records on Hatonn.

SOLAR SYSTEM 22—Another Solar System containing 22 Planets.

SOLAS—The Sun.

SOLEX MAL—The original language once spoken on Earth; the mother-tongue; the Solar-tongue; spoken by all people of Outer Space; a symbolic, pictographic language.

SUTTKU—Judge of the Saturn Council.

TERRA—From the Planet Venus; on Ship 4.

TIME-KEEPERS—A group that computes Cycles.

TONAS—Musical instruments.

TORESOTON—Another Solar System.

TOURA—From Pluto.

TROCTON—A spaceship of the Solar X Group.

UM—From Mars; wife of Zo.

VEC—Space in the Solex Mal.

WAN-4—Representative of the Safanian Solar System.

ZAGO—A member of a contact group; from Mars.

ZO—From Neptune; Head of a Masar contact group.

ZRS—From Uranus.

TESTING ONE, TWO, THREE. . .
ESTABLISHING CONTACT WITH YOUR
FRIENDLY ULTRA-TERRESTRIAL

By Sean Casteel

Tim Beckley says there is much more to the well worn cliché "ET Phone Home" than most UFOlogists would suspect. To some, it is more than just a phrase lifted from the movie "ET, The Extraterrestrial." It has almost become a way of life for those who believe it is within the realm of possibility to communicate with "them," whomever "they" might be.

For you see, Conspiracy Journal/Inner Light publisher Timothy Green Beckley doesn't like to refer to the UFOnauts as "aliens," because he doesn't want to have to pigeonhole who they are or where they might be from. To him, this is still a matter of open debate and conjecture. To veteran saucer buffs, the idea that all UFO related phenomena are interplanetary in origin casts a shadow over the entire field and makes some in the media and in the scientific community think we are quacks looking to promote an unlikely idea without adequate proof.

In a previous article, as well as a book I co-authored with Beckley about two years ago, I found myself struggling with the notion that we are primarily dealing with a celestial component. I had been "raised" to believe that flying saucers were from outer space. After all, hasn't this been the most popular theory, dating back to the days of Major Donald E. Keyhoe and Frank Edwards? Weren't there UFO crashes to consider? Close encounters with all sorts of humanoids that had to be from "out there?" And dozens of reports from pilots who said they were chased and encircled? What other explanation could there be for all of these shenanigans?

My research for the book _Our Alien Planet: This Eerie Earth_ pointed me in a slightly different direction, and it is easy to see where a person's mind could easily be blown by the ample amount of evidence that the "aliens" might be a different type of life form, but that they don't necessarily have to have a cosmic link, that they could originate from a place a lot closer to home than the Pleiades, for example. I even went further out on a limb with my contribution to the volume _The Secret Space Program: Who Is Responsible_?

In my earlier article, I spoke candidly about the idea that what we typically call "aliens" may instead be a catch-all phrase for beings or entities or energies who originate from somewhere on or closer to Earth and have perhaps dwelled alongside man and guided him, for good or evil, since ancient times. In this continuation, the subject will be communicating with the Ultra-Terrestrials, which is what Beckley calls the "aliens," although he admits that he did not originate the term. He says through trial and error it is possible to learn how to converse with the obviously more advanced and ever mysterious race on a one-to-one basis. (Naturally, there could be more than one "source" we find ourselves dealing with).

This idea is the focus of the second half of Timothy Green Beckley's recent book, "_The Authentic Book of Ultra-Terrestrial Contacts,_" which offers several methods for and stories about actually "speaking" to the as-yet-undefined entities.

"A lot of people," Beckley said, "who don't realize that communicating with the Ultra-Terrestrials is a two-way street, tend to poke fun at and act skeptically toward someone like Stephen Greer, who claims the 'unique' ability to wander out into a field or the open desert and aim a flashlight toward the sky and seemingly get a response from 'something or other' that may be hovering unseen nearby."

But, according to Beckley, what Greer claims is unique is really something not that unusual in the annals of Ufology. Beckley said that the intelligence behind or inside these vessels – and he tends not to want to use the word 'vehicles,' as that would indicate a solid structure of some type, where in reality these objects may be anything from living, breathing energy pods to beings from another dimension or even a breakaway civilization which we haven't been able to identify – has been communicating with various "contactees" since the early 1950s.

He cites the case of George Hunt Williamson, one of the original witnesses to legendary contactee George Adamski's contacts with the Space Brother known as "Orthon." Williamson spent years speaking with the Ultra-Terrestrials over a ham radio and eventually wrote a book called "The Saucers Speak." Beckley has republished Williamson's book as "Other Voices," available on Amazon.com or from the publisher himself.

REACHING OUT TO HELPFUL STRANGERS

Returning to Beckley's book, "The Authentic Book of Ultra-Terrestrial Contacts," we come to a chapter called "The Principles of Motive and Desire," in which a spiritual messenger named Tuella (Earth name Thelma Terrell) offers instructions on how to contact the "guardians," or benevolent Ultra-Terrestrials trying to guide mankind's development. Tuella claims this message was channeled through her by an entity named "Andromeda Rex," the commander of a fleet of spaceships now circling the Earth, part of an off-world or interdimensional operation known as the Ashtar Command.

There are, according to Tuella, five basic requirements for successful contact between our dimensions, both on a conscious and telepathic level.

"First," Tuella begins, "I would list 'Qualification of Motive.' What is the motive or desire? The desire must stand clean and undefiled by any self-centered purpose. The motive must be totally free of any desire for self-aggrandizement or the flaunting of self above others."

Another negative factor that would hinder the communication is that the person seeking contact must not be "launching a program that would return gain or fame to the souls so seeking." Wrong motivation will stop any seeker "in their tracks."

The second condition, Tuella says, is to "Let Dedication be the inspiration which directs the heart in our direction." One must have a selfless dedication to mankind as a whole and to the uplifting of the plant into its fourth dimensional expression and the fulfillment of the Aquarian Age on Earth.

"Those whose hearts bleed for the spiritual needs of humanity," according to Andromeda Rex, "and are dedicated to the coming of the Kingdom of God on Earth, register our attention automatically."

The next basic requirement is something Andromeda Rex calls "Consecration," the act of Love and Surrender of the human spirit to a Divine Purpose.

"Love is the strongest element in the universe," he says, "and the highest possible vibration on your planet. It shines upon our monitoring boards like diamonds across a dark sky." Those who vibrate a life of love to all people of all worlds will not be ignored in the great scheme of things. Those who lift their loving thoughts to the Ultra-Terrestrials will receive their love in return.

The fourth condition is called "Concentration," and Andromeda Rex promises that those who concentrate on the Ultra-Terrestrials and their "ships" with love and a peaceful, quiet mind will be monitored and their discipline in this regard will be duly noted with a loving reward.

And finally, Andromeda Rex calls attention to "Meditation," achieving a quiet, tranquil state of mind. Into this beautiful quietude "will come the still, small voice of heavenly response."

"Following these exercises," Tuella adds, "one always gives thanks for that quiet moment spent with inner divinity, whatever its results may or may not have been."

It sounds like the Ultra-Terrestrials are looking for a very specialized sort of person, and that only the completely unselfish and lovingly motivated need apply. It may be that one is required to attain a state of being close to sainthood before communicating with the Ultra-Terrestrials, but it is nevertheless comforting to know that Tuella's Andromeda Rex intends us no harm and that meeting his requirements would not involve anything immoral or degrading.

Beckley admits in personal conversations that to his way of thinking these types of communication seems a bit preachy or New Age-ie for his liking.

"After all," he says, "in these communications, you really don't know who might be channeling through you or what their ulterior motives might be. But it's catchy and it's nice to think that some other intelligence might have our well being – and not just their own – at heart!"

JANE ALLYSON AND TELEPATHIC CONTACT

Jane Allyson's stories of telepathic contact with the Ultra-Terrestrials are also included in Beckley's book. Until the Fourth of July in 1979, Jane had never had the slightest interest in UFOs – then the unexpected happened! While standing with two other people on a New York City rooftop, waiting for a fireworks display to begin, Jane and her companions saw a brightly lit object against a darkened sky.

As the object moved closer, Jane and the others could make out a definite shape, like a huge diamond star glowing in the night. She was anxious for the ship to move closer and give them all a better view of this unworldly vehicle. Jane had prior experience with meditating, and she began to lead those present in a Native-American chant, which lasted for several minutes.

The object continued to come nearer until they thought it was preparing to land on the rooftop. Jane felt fear and awe at the same time, and was forced to wonder if the object was going to sweep her and her companions off the roof or even crush them beneath its weight. Just when it seemed they might all break apart from the psychological pressure, the object disappeared.

Later, in the apartment of one of Jane's friends, some odd after-effects took place. One of the witnesses began to dance around the room as if hearing some inner music. The other person began to meditate for the first time in his life. Meanwhile, Jane felt a tremendous sense of compassion moving through her body, "producing such a powerful feeling of love for the entire human race, making me feel more alive than I had ever felt before."

Jane believes that whoever was aboard the "diamond" in the sky could mentally hear her and her companions chanting.

"They recognized the fact," she said, "that we were altering our consciousness, lifting our vibrations so that our bodies and minds were operating more in their dimension."

THE NATIVE-AMERICAN WAY

Beckley's late friend, the Native American Bleu Ocean, once told Beckley that chanting has long been a means for Bleu's people to communicate with the Ultra-Terrestrials.

"Our ancestors had special chants just for that purpose," Bleu, who was a musician who worked with such rock pop stars as Pink Floyd, said. "They communicated with 'star people' on a regular basis and knew a lot more about the workings of the solar system than modern man is led to believe."

Bleu added that when contact was being attempted, his forefathers never wore anything made of metal. They dressed simply and carried nothing that might counteract the polarity of a hovering "spaceship." Wearing anything metal might accidentally pull them into the electrical field of the craft and injure them.

JOHN OTTO'S "LIGHT BEAM COMMUNICATOR"

Down through the years, there have been several attempts to construct a machine that can take communication with the Ultra-Terrestrials to a whole new level beyond the vagaries of telepathic contact. Chicagoan John Otto made such an effort in the early 1950s when he invented a device called a "light-beam communicator."

"Without claiming 'firsts' in any effort," Otto said, "for we find wherever we turn there is nothing new under the sun, it was nevertheless the sighting of a large cigar-shaped craft near Needles, California, that spurred me into thinking of a radical new means of a communication attempt. Feeling rather stupid after shining a flashlight skyward while snuggled in a bedroll in the desert that night, the idea of light-beam communication was born for interplanetary use."

The device was relatively cheap to build and fairly simple in design. It connected a microphone, into which he could speak, to a power pack and a bright searchlight. A converter turned Otto's voice into vibrating shafts of light that could be picked up on-board a spaceship.

A friend of Otto's, who often went with the inventor into the desert to attempt contact with the UFOs seen frequently there, said that one night success came shortly after midnight.

"This giant craft appeared overhead," his friend said, "and Otto started talking into his device. The beam from the light beam communicator struck the metal hull of the spaceship and the air was filled with a slight humming noise as the UFO seemed to acknowledge our presence. The ship tilted slightly back and forth as if whoever was inside was attempting to respond. In those days, Otto had not perfected a receiver to pick up messages from flying saucers, but later on I understand that he did."

Otto liked to tell a funny story about a friend of his who had been going outdoors on a regular basis with a light-beam communicator he had built using schematic diagrams drawn up by Otto.

"He was continuously modulating canned music," Otto recounted, "and sending out a jumbled collection of words, always closing with, 'How is my readability?' After several weeks, he had a reception of the same type of material: jumbled, unintelligible words and then some music. Finally came, 'How is my readability?' My friend did not have anything of importance ready to converse with his unseen communicator, so it floored him somewhat. This is why you should consider in advance any plans to transmit."

The parroting back of Otto's friend's jumbled transmissions by the Ultra-Terrestrials may have been intended as humorous, to turn the tables, so to speak, on the innocuous yet frivolous waste of time he had burdened them with.

Beckley points out that, although Otto may not have realized it, the original plans for the light-beam communicator may have been sent to him telepathically by the Ultra-Terrestrials. While Otto would later patent the device as his own, it may take its place among the many "New Age" inventions that are psychically beamed to Earth by the Space Brothers to jumpstart the contact process. Certainly other variations on Otto's light-beam communicator have been developed independently from his that still held true to its basic design.

Meanwhile, who remembers "Raiders of the Lost Ark"? Toward the end of the movie, one of the Nazi villains explains why Hitler is so determined to find the Ark of the Covenant. "It is a radio for talking to God," the wickedly grinning Nazi says. Was Moses also similarly instructed on building a kind of light-beam communicator? Are the Ultra-Terrestrials trying to make conversation with our Creator a simple matter of flipping an on switch and speaking into a microphone?

NO JOKING AROUND FOR THE MITCHELL SISTERS

Beckley goes on to talk about two sisters, Helen and Betty Mitchell, who not only had a face-to-face meeting with a pair of Ultra-Terrestrials, but were also instructed on how to build a communications device for secret contact with the mysterious though human-appearing race. The incident happened in a St. Louis coffee shop in the late 1950s.

The two sisters had been out shopping and decided to refresh themselves with a soft drink. They were approached "in a very mannerly way" by two gentlemen dressed in suits who interrupted the sisters' private conversation. The two interlopers said they were from a huge mother-craft orbiting the Earth and that their names were Elen and Zelas. The two sisters were informed that they had been under careful watch since their birth and were shocked when they were told stories about themselves that only other family members could have known.

The sisters were "chosen," the gentlemen said, to serve as channels so that certain information could be given to the people of the Earth. The girls were amazed by what they heard, and felt the intruders radiated kindness, warmth and wisdom. They Ultra-Terrestrials said they would return and contact the sisters again.

A week later, the two sisters felt impelled to return to the same coffee shop and this time they encountered just one of the Ultra-Terrestrials. He gave the sisters instructions for building a device that would allow them to contact the Ultra-Terrestrials.

"His instructions were explicit and precise," Helen Mitchell said later, "for he warned us that unless we placed every piece of the device in the proper place we would not be able to contact them with it. We were not allowed to take the drawn diagram of the device with us, but we had to remember it as it was explained to us. When we obtained the proper pieces for the device, we constructed it when we returned home, and were happy to find the results were satisfactory."

To their amazement, the girls were able to speak with the same person they had seen earlier. Over the next six months, they spoke many times with the Ultra-Terrestrials and learned a great deal about their home, sciences and spacecraft.

A later incident happened when Helen was alone in downtown St. Louis. She was contacted by the Ultra-Terrestrials and asked to drive to a heavily wooded area. She next boarded one of their scout craft and was flown to a large mother ship, where she was taken on a tour. Helen was shown the room where she and her sister's calls were received, and the aliens even placed a call to the sisters' home in St. Louis and allowed Helen to speak to Betty and tell her she was with "the brothers." Helen was also shown an aerial view of their home right inside, as though the roof and the ceiling had been magically removed. She could see her sister, mother and the younger children moving around.

Helen and Betty Mitchell had many more contacts, according to Beckley, but they soon dropped out of the picture, deciding to keep their experiences to themselves because of the fear of possible ridicule. Their whereabouts are unknown today, although they are more than likely deceased, since this episode goes back several decades. Apparently, their communications with the Ultra-Terrestrials even sparked an interest by the CIA, who started to "meddle into their business," either to spread disinformation about the case or to see if the sisters' claims to have established a communications link might have been legitimate. Hell, why did the aliens speak to them and not the government?

TIM BECKLEY HIMSELF ATTEMPTS CONTACT

Not to be outdone by those he writes about, Tim Beckley himself has a story to tell about attempting to contact the Ultra-Terrestrials.

In the early 1980s, while in the U.K. to speak before an unofficial UFO discussion group at the House of Lords (a meeting organized by the 8th Earl of Clancarty, Brinsley Le Poer Trench, who was himself an originator of the ancient astronauts theory of UFOs), Beckley took a side trip to the small English town of Warminster, located on the heels of Salisbury Plain and Stonehenge in the southwest part of England.

"Warminster had been a UFO hotbed for quite a while before I got there," Beckley said. "According to local testimony, it all began on a Christmas morning in 1964 when a pensioner on her way to church heard this horrific sound coming from all around her that sounded like a million bees buzzing. She soon found herself pressed to the ground by an invisible force. The sound was tied in with the sightings of various UFOs, which plagued the town for years and years."

The sightings were concentrated around three hills in the area: Cradle Hill, Starr Hill and Cley Hill. All three hills had a history of unexplainable phenomena associated with them, including crop circles a century or more before the term was coined.

Beckley had been corresponding with Arthur Shuttlewood, the editor of the "*Warminster Journal*," who regularly published local UFO reports but remained a skeptic himself.

That is, until Shuttlewood had a few sightings of his own, and became part of a regular series of sky-watches in the area, some of which were attended by celebrities like Mick Jagger and David Bowie. Some attendees felt that open contact had been established. On several occasions, the editor had beamed a powerful flashlight into the heavens that actually bounced a ray off the hull of a craft. Whoever was inside would seem to sway in the sky as if acknowledging his attempt to say hello.

Beckley arrived in Warminster and had lunch with the newspaperman and his sky-watch companion, a retired RAF pilot named Bob Strong, who showed Beckley a scrapbook filled with literally dozens of UFO photos showing craft of all shapes and sizes, from "railroad cars," to huge, bat-like objects.

That night, Beckley and his compatriots saw several meteors streak across their line of vision. Around 10 P.M., they spotted something fairly high up that seemed to just

be hovering above them. Shuttlewood went to the trunk of his car and pulled out his trusty flashlight, then pointed it at the object and flashed a light several times. He then offered the flashlight to Beckley, who also flashed it at the object.

"The reaction was tremendous," Beckley recalled. "Every time we blinked at it, the UFO would sort of swing back and forth, like a pendulum would. It seemed to be looking down on us. Maybe it picked up our thoughts telepathically. I was told to keep a positive mind because that's what the Ultra-Terrestrials seemed to respond to the most."

The sky-watch went on for another 20 minutes or so and then it started to rain and clouds obscured the group's view. When they saw nothing more, they retired for the evening.

"Had I made contact with a UFO?" Beckley still wonders. "I will never know for sure, but it did seem as if the object was under intelligent control and was responding to our request to prove it was not just an 'ordinary object' in the heavens. Another strange thing: We took several photos of Cradle Hill that night. When developed, one of them showed a strange phenomenon behind two of the witnesses – streaks or bolts of light which were not visible to the naked eye at the time and for which there is no explanation. There were no streetlamps or houses with porch lights nearby."

For historical purposes we hereby provide an audio link provided to a public statement made by Arthur Shuttlewood at the time of all the Warminster hoopla.

https://www.box.com/shared/4hki2zkhnk#/s/4hki2zkhnk/1/23529576/248084286/1

DOING THE COMMUNICATION THING YOURSELF

"*The Authentic Book of Ultra-Terrestrial Contacts*" even includes instructions on building your own light-beam communicator, complete with schematic diagrams. But one should approach such communication attempts with caution, the book warns. You definitely want to make contact with the righteous side of "the Force," to use an expression from the "Star Wars" movies.

The reality of the situation is that there are forces out there that do not

have mankind's best interests at heart. As Tuella warns in her channeled message from Andromeda Rex, spiritual purity and love on the part of the seeker are required to make contact with the forces of good.

It's been said that talking to God is perfectly fine, but if you hear him answer back, you've got problems. Hopefully that is not the case when it comes to communicating with the Ultra-Terrestrials. Perhaps there really are ways to establish voice contact with virtual angels, either telepathically or with the aid of a communicating device made according to instructions from the ones above. Any resulting conversations could be the salvation of us all.

* * * * * * * *

SUGGESTED READING

The Authentic Book Of Ultra-Terrestrial Contacts by Timothy Beckley

https://www.box.com/shared/4hki2zkhnk#/s/4hki2zkhnk/1/23529576/248084286/1

Our Alien Planet: This Eerie Earth by Timothy Beckley and Sean Casteel

http://www.amazon.com/Our-Alien-Planet-Eerie-Earth/dp/1892062887/ref=sr_1_1?s=books&ie=UTF8&qid=1344733442&sr=1-1&keywords=our+alien+planet+beckley

The Secret Space Program: Who Is Responsible?

By Beckley, Casteel, Tim Swartz and Commander X

http://www.amazon.com/Secret-Space-Program-Responsible-Civilization/dp/1606111094/ref=sr_1_1?s=books&ie=UTF8&qid=1344733572&sr=1-1&keywords=Secret+Space+Program++beckley

* * * * * * * * * *

[If you enjoyed this article, visit Sean Casteel's "UFO Journalist" website at www.seancasteel.com]

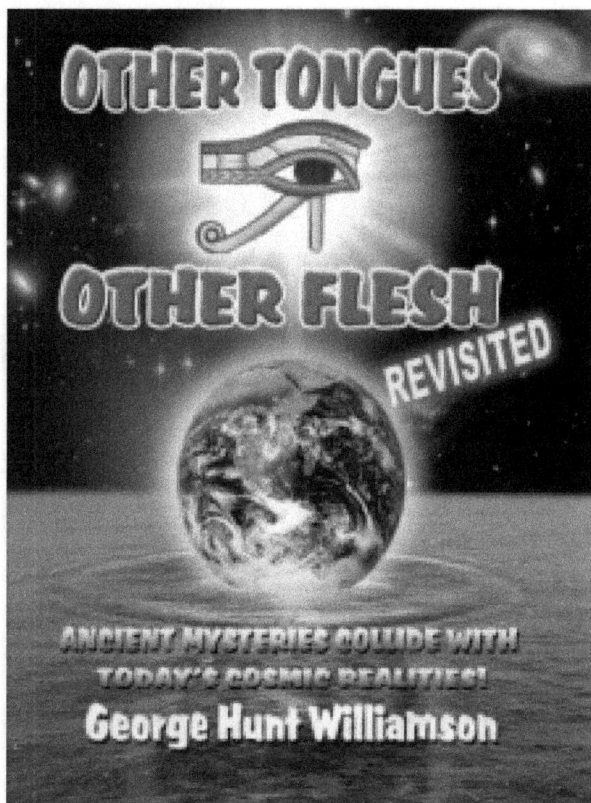

OTHER TONGUES OTHER FLESH REVISITED

By George Hunt Williamson - Edited by Timothy Green Beckley

"IN MY HOUSE THERE ARE MANY MANSIONS," JESUS STATED. NOW HERE IS THE PROOF!

"Evidence has accumulated that there are people on earth that don't really belong here!" George Hunt Williamson, author of *OTHER TONGUES OTHER FLESH* stated as early as 1955.

This doesn't mean they came here aboard a flying saucer, disembarked, put on a tweed suit, polished up their earthly languages and moved into the house next door. It does mean, however that there is a special class or order of beings in the Universe that are different from us because of the fact that they must wander from one world to another, and from one place to another. They are the "chimney sweeps" of creation. It is their specific job to be the "trash cans" of the Universe and aid their fellow man on these backward worlds."

They come in many disguises. . . Most are friendly. A few are NOT! They include: THE WANDERERS; THE MIGRANTS; THE PROPHETS; THE HARVESTERS; THE AGENTS; THE INTRUDERS; THE GUESSERS.

In *OTHER TONGUES OTHER FLESH REVISITED*, Williamson deciphers the strange symbols left from a depression of the bottom of the spaceman's shoes in the soil from which a plaster of paris cast was made on the spot. This is the famous George Adamski contact with Orthon in the desert of which Williamson was the primary witness.

Here are SECRETS concerning the creation of life and the evolution of humankind entrusted to only a handful. And, although Williamson has passed on, his legacy is vastly important. So much so that Alec Hidel in the Excluded Middle recently confided: "There can be no doubt that, by accident or design, Williamson and his various collaborators played an enormous part in shaping New Age thought in all its manifestations. Together they constituted the single most important occult group of the post-war era. Their influence is made all the more remarkable by the fact that it has seldom been acknowledged, or even perceived by other researchers in the field."

$24.00 + $5.00 s/h from:
Timothy Beckley • Box 753 • New Brunswick, NJ 08903
FREE SUBSCRIPTION www.ConspiracyJournal.Com

Ancient Astronauts And The Ultra-Terrestrials

The Revealed Truth Could Cause Worldwide Religious, Political And Energy Upheavals!

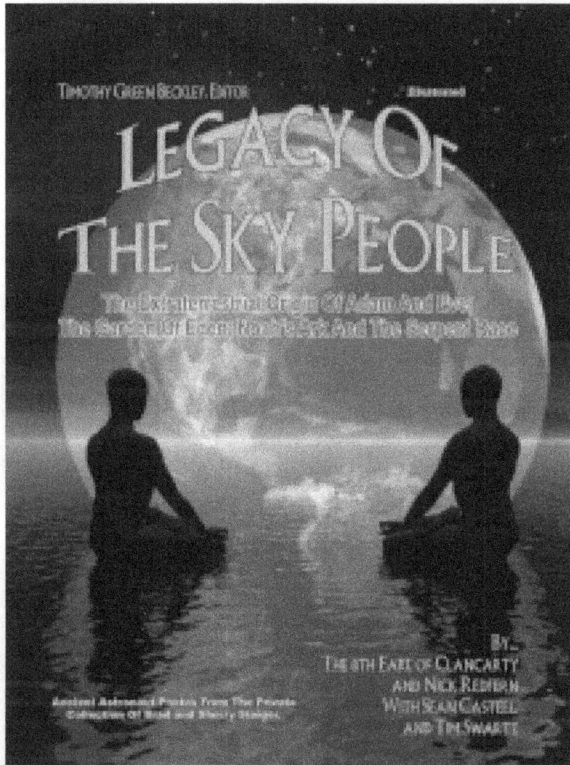

The belief in strange beings coming down from the stars to intermingle with humanity can be traced back to the earliest days of mankind. While the scientific community maintains that the current notion of UFOs and their extraterrestrial pilots is simply a modern version of the myths and legends contained within almost every culture and civilization, Ancient Astronaut theorists maintain that we have been "tinkered with," and that someone – or "something" else – is keeping a watchful eye over mankind for their own purposes, purposes we can only speculate about at present.

As early as the 1960s, Britain's 8th Earl of Clancarty, Brinsley Le Poer Trench, made an astounding revelation. He said that he was convinced that life on Earth had originated on the planet Mars and that the first voyagers here had been the Biblical Adam and Eve, who had left the paradise of the Garden of Eden and arrived on Earth in a space ark piloted by Noah. Thus the roots of the various Biblical stories from the Old Testament began to grow and blossom, stories which are taught in every Sunday school today.

But the stories told by this paragon of British nobility and the other researchers in this book combine to form an even a stranger tale about the secret history of our planet, a history that is "forbidden knowledge" held by a handful of individuals who are now sharing their findings for the first time:

˙ Why has the CIA and the military shown an unprecedented interest in the remains of what many claim to be Noah's Ark, now resting on Turkey's Mount Ararat? Is the anomalous structure a crashed space ship, something metallic as opposed to the gopher-wood of the Biblical tale, as researcher Nick Redfern insists could be true?

˙ Is there a distinction to be made between the ancient aliens and the true Creator God, and do these "visitors" have the same imponderable questions as we do about life, death and religion? Eric von Daniken spokesman Giorgio Tsoukalos has his own ideas on this concept.

˙ "We have met the Martians and they are us," suggests Brad Steiger. Is there new evidence to suggest that life on Earth was first planted in South America and spread out from there?

˙ Is there a new race of humans being formed in these uncertain times? According to the Earl of Clancarty, some of us are rapidly reacquiring the telepathy and psychic abilities we were originally created with.

125

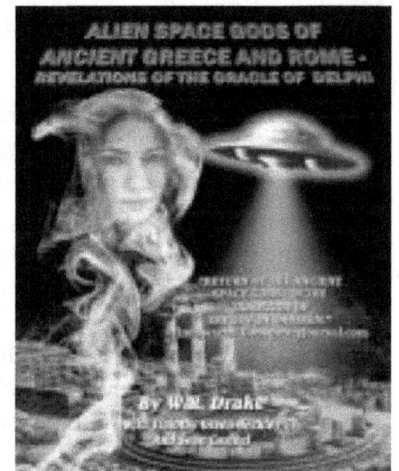

www.ingramcontent.com/pod-product-compliance
Lightning Source LLC
Chambersburg PA
CBHW062103090426
42741CB00015B/3316

* 9 7 8 1 6 0 6 1 1 1 3 2 1 *